The S

The Storyteller Collection

The Storyteller Collection

The Storyteller Collection

Marie Browders

The Storyteller Collection

The Storyteller Collection

King Solomon once said...
"What has been will be again,
what has been done will be done again;
there is nothing new under the sun."
Ecclesiastes 1:9 NIV

Copyright © 2017 Marie Browders

All rights reserved.

ISBN: 1542683068
ISBN 13: 9781542683067
Library of Congress Control Number: **XXXXX (If applicable)**
LCCN Imprint Name: **City and State (If applicable)**

The Storyteller Collection

Table of Contents

Stay! 7

The Call 25

The Murdered 45

The Promise 71

Telling Lies 95

The Friend 121

Words 145

The Relative 173

Seeking Justice 195

The Seven 211

The Winding Road 257

Home 279

The Storyteller Collection

The Storyteller Collection

The Storyteller Collection

Stay!

The child slammed the door to her bedroom and threw herself on the bed; she was just fuming. She didn't understand why her parents wouldn't let her go to her friend's older brother's party! Her parents said that her friend's brother was too old for her to hang out with, but her friend would be at the party, too, and they were the same age. It was so unfair!

And though she was fifteen, her friend's brother was only nineteen. She pleaded with her parents that possibly her friend's parents would be there…maybe.

She then began to envision that everyone at school was going to think she was a baby because she was not allowed to go. She was not a baby, and she didn't want her parents to control her life anymore!

She was going to that party! She got off her bed, seated herself in front of her computer, and quickly sent her friend a message that she would be coming to the party after all. Then, she was going to run away!

Her friend exclaimed that it was so exciting and that she would be waiting for her.

Now that she had formalized an impetuous plan, she began to go around her room, stuffing things into a backpack. She instinctively grabbed her teddy bear and then thought better of it, as she was now grown; she would not take babyish things like teddy bears with her. The child felt a little sad leaving her favorite teddy bear behind, but there was simply no room for it.

Her backpack was now full, and she was waiting for her home to settle down so that she could sneak out. Minutes felt like hours, but finally, the house was all quiet.

The girl eased out of her bedroom and slowly headed toward the front door. She noticed her mother's purse lying there on a table by the front door and realized she had no money.

She opened her mom's purse and took all the money she could find in it—thirty-four dollars. She then eased out the front door, closing it quietly.

The Storyteller Collection

It was quite dark outside, and the cool, crisp air encircled her. She pulled her thin coat closer around her small frame; oh, how had she wished she had brought her heavier coat instead of this light, flimsy one! She glanced back at the front door of her house and thought of going back and getting her warmer coat but decided not to, as she was afraid of getting caught by her parents. So she pulled her thin coat tightly about her, pulled her backpack over her shoulders, and rushed into the night air.

Her friend only lived six blocks away, but it was dark and creepy outside, and she seemed to hear so many spooky sounds; for a brief instant, she thought of just going back home. Then, she remembered the altercation she had had with her mother, and a new resolve enveloped her as she trudged on to her friend's house.

In the distance, she could faintly hear sounds of the party. When she was about a half block away, sounds of music enveloped her. She began to get excited then! As she drew closer, she began to see other kids going toward the party, so she fell in with them.

The Storyteller Collection

"Hi." She looked to her right and saw an unusually dressed young man in clothing from the medieval period. His hair was dark and curly; however, he appeared no older than herself.

"Hello." She smiled and continued toward the party.

"Greetings. May I ask your name?" he asked her as he walked alongside her.

"Oh, just call me Freedom!" she said flippantly. "I'm finally free of my parents' control."

"Interesting. In my day, I, too, bristled against my father's control over me."

"So, you know how I feel," she said. "My parents told me that I could not go to this party because I was too young. I was so angry at my parents. All they want to do is try to run my life! But I showed them; after the party, I am going to run away. That will teach them!"

"Tell me, will it teach them—or you?" the young man questioned. "So, what are you going to do after the party? What are your plans?"

"I haven't thought that far ahead. I will probably stay with my friend for the night."

"Is she going to let you stay? Will her parents allow that?"

"Like I said, I hadn't given it much thought." The girl was irritated now. All she wanted to do was get to the party. She would think of what she would do afterward.

"You sound just like me." He shook his head, smiling. "I had an older brother once who was always doing as he was told and admonishing me for my lagging ways, which frequently annoyed me. I wanted to leave home, but, in order for me to do this, I needed my inheritance from my father so that I could go my own way." "I pestered my father for my inheritance day in and day out, until he was at his wits' end and decided to give me my share of my inheritance. When he finally did that, I was on top of the world. I felt like I was then in control of my own destiny."

The girl and the young man were quite close to the party now. More and more young people were showing up.

The Storyteller Collection

She then asked the young man, "So, what did you do?"

"I felt that I knew more about how to lead my own life, so I left home." There was a bench in the front yard,

and they seated themselves on it to continue their conversation.

"I remembered how I felt as I was on the road, heading toward my destiny. I thought, 'No one will ever tell me what to do again.' I thought of myself as a man, although, in actuality, I was just a teenager.

"Like you, I didn't think when I left my father's house; I just reacted. I was ill-prepared to take care of myself. I know my father still had more instruction to bestow upon me, but I did not want it; that was my first mistake.

"The first thing that happened to me was that I was swindled out of some of my inheritance, because I was not well-prepared to look out for thieves, such as the ones I encountered. If I had continued my education from my father and older brother, I would not have been victimized.

"But, since I still had a fair amount of my inheritance left, I didn't pay that much attention to my loss. That was my second mistake, as I did not learn from this encounter, and I did not take measures to ensure that this would not happen again.

"I have to admit that I was not a good steward of my inheritance, which was my final mistake. I continued to squander the remainder of my inheritance on wine, women, and a loose lifestyle. I partied and fizzled away the balance of my inheritance until it was all gone. In my delusional state and my immaturity, I felt I would never run out of my inheritance—but I was so wrong."

The girl thought of the thirty-six dollars, which she had taken from her mother's purse. "But you seem like you have it together now. I mean, you got your act together."

"Yes, I did get my act together, as you would say," Agreed the young man, "but not before I had squandered all that I had. I woke one day after partying to find that I had no money left. People were then unwilling to assist me, as that is what family does, not strangers.

The Storyteller Collection

"I had to obtain employment—fast! Since I was uneducated, the only position I found was cleaning out pig stalls. It was a deplorable situation: smelly, hot, and tiring. I finally came to my senses and realized how narrow-minded and selfish I had become. My father and my brother were offering me life's lessons for free; they were teaching me things from which I would obtain wisdom and with which I could better maneuver life. But I acted like a petulant child, constantly complaining over being told what to do.

"I began to wish for the life I had known at my father's home. The servants there were treated much better than I was here. So, with a heavy heart and defeated attitude, I decided to return to my father's home and beg for forgiveness and a job, not as a son but as their servant.

"Day and night, I traveled, until I came upon my father's house. Seeing it in the distance truly warmed my heart. But soon, trepidation sank in, as I wondered if they would even allow me to work for them.

"My father looked up, saw me, and began to jump with glee! I bowed before my father saying, 'F-father, I have sinned against you and against God.

The Storyteller Collection

I am no longer worthy to be called your son. I beg of you, make me like one of your servants, and I shall serve you all the days of my life.'

"My father had tears in his eyes as he said to his servants, 'Quick, bring my best robe and put it on my son. Put a ring on his finger and sandals on his feet. Go take a fattened calf, and kill it. Let's feast and celebrate for this son of mine who was dead and is alive again; he was lost and now is found!'" He was referencing Luke 15:22.

"I couldn't believe how generous my father was with his forgiveness of me. However, though my father was happy to see me, my brother was not. When he came home from the fields, he heard music and dancing. He motioned to one of the servants to find out what had occurred while he was working; he was told, 'Your brother has come, and your father has killed the fattened calf to celebrate his safe return.'

"My older brother was angry and would not enter the house. My father went out to speak to him, and my brother exploded, saying, 'Look, all these years I've been slaving for you, and I never disobeyed your orders, Yet you have never given me even a young goat so that I could celebrate with my friends. But when this son of yours, who has squandered your property with prostitutes, comes home, you celebrate him!'

"'Oh, my son,' my father said to my oldest brother, 'it is well known that you are always with me, and everything I have is yours. You are the wiser of the two of you, for you took my counsel and heeded all of my teachings. Your brother did not; he had to go into the world to find his wisdom. He has lost all his inheritance in order to gain his insight. Because of this, I feared he was dead, but he came home with wisdom he did not have when he left, so I say that your brother was dead, but now, he is alive! In his foolish heart, he was lost to us—mentally, spiritually, and emotionally—but now, in all that he has gained, he has managed to gain wisdom as well.'

"My brother finally got it, and so did I. Though I had lost my inheritance, I gained something far more valuable: maturity, insight, and wisdom."

"But I can't go back to my parent's house!" she said, as his story sank into her. "They treated me like a child and refused to let me have any fun."

"Well, if 'fun' is your endeavor, then why haven't you gone in to the party? Why are you sitting on a bench in the yard?"

The Storyteller Collection

"W-well, we were talking. I am going to go."

"In your search for pleasure, you've not thought of the dangers that lie ahead of this poorly planned adventure. In your stubbornness, you don't realize that Satan is trying to take your life. In your anger, you haven't realized that you are a young child, alone on the streets and with no thought of tomorrow.

"That is why God gave you parents to lead and guide you until you can do it for yourself. Parents are there to keep you safe and instill wisdom in you so that you can navigate in this world alone. When parents say 'no,' they are, in actuality, telling you that they love you enough to even fight you for you! They want you to know that 'no' doesn't mean 'no' forever; it just means 'no' until you are old enough and wise enough to discern the wisdom they are imparting to you. So many children make fateful decisions that literally cost them their lives.

"Here are some examples for you: A fifteen-year-old ran away to be with a boy she met. The two were hitchhiking and encountered a truck driver who killed the boy, then raped and slaughtered the girl. One other child accepted a ride with a stranger. After he raped her, he chopped off her arms! It was by the grace of God that this child lived, and she now speaks across the country to teens about the perils of not listening to her parents."

"You are just trying to scare me." The girl shivered.

"No," contradicted the young man, "Parents are well aware of the dangers; that's why they take your requests, evaluate the situations (not just the 'fun' parts) and, with their wisdom of foreseeing possible negative outcomes, they make decisions that may not be popular with you, but it's not their job to win a popularity contest. They are parenting their children.

"My father knew of the dangers that lay ahead of my inexperience of the world, and he thought I had died because of my bad judgment. He was astonished that I came home; I was broke but wiser and, more importantly, alive."

"But I can't go back home," the girl said. "I know my mother will be angry with me and will ground me forever!"

"Well, you will have to earn their trust back, I agree, and you can do that, in time. Just be honest, and don't lie to them. Tell them the truth of how you felt and how your anger clouded your judgment temporarily, but, once you walked out in the air and cooled down, you realized that they were only doing this for your benefit.

The Storyteller Collection

"While you're walking back home, ask God to forgive you for your stubborn nature. Ask Him to cover you with His blood and to keep you safe from harm. Implore Him to instill in you wisdom, of which you are sorely lacking, to lead and guide you all the days of your life. Trust me when I tell you that He will do it!"

"Well I am getting cold...maybe I should go home."

"An excellent idea! I will walk you home myself."

She did not take the time to say good-bye to her friend; she didn't even go into the party, as she now realized that it wasn't the party for her.

Going back home didn't seem so scary, now that she had someone to walk with her. She was home in no time.

Her house was just as she had left it: quiet and dark. She turned toward the boy and smiled.

"Well, this is my house. Thanks for walking me home. Are you going back to the party?"

"No. I have to go down to Maple Street to intercept another youngster who is sneaking out of his house for a different kind of adventure."

"Oh, do you go around saving all to whom you speak?"

"No," he shook his head, "but not for the lack of trying. You see, this is my calling. I am the prodigal son, and my calling is not to stop people from running away; it is to remind them how to find their ways home."

He smiled at her and waved as she scurried into her house.

End

The Storyteller Collection

So many children get entangled in things that are out of their control, but the Lord lays His hands on them and sends a protector with a story of his own to remind them which way home is. He is the prodigal son, who has lessons to reveal and stories to be told.

News Story #1

Robert Ben Rhoades became notorious for the truck he drove. He converted the sleeper cab into his own personal torture chamber. Rhoades is believed to have first killed in November of 1989, though he was only accused by one unnamed victim of kidnapping and torture. Even then, when Rhoades was detained, the victim denied that he was the perpetrator. It was later asserted that she was fearful of Rhoades after enduring two weeks in his torture chamber.

Rhoades' first confirmed victims were Candace Walsh and her husband, Douglas Zyskowski, in January of 1990. The couple was hitchhiking. Rhoades picked them up in his truck while on a long-haul journey. He immediately killed Zyskowski and dumped his body in Sutton County,

Texas (midway between San Antonio and El Paso), where it was later found; however, the body was not identified until 1992. Rhoades kept Walsh for over a week. During this time, he tortured and raped her multiple times before dumping her body in Millard County, Utah.

A month after Walsh's death, fourteen-year-old Regina Kay Walters and her boyfriend, Ricky Lee Jones, ran away from the Houston suburb of Pasadena, Texas. As with Zyskowski, it is believed that, after being picked up by Rhoades, Jones was killed and disposed of, while Walters was kept. Photos seized during a search of the home of Rhoades when he was later arrested confirmed that he held Regina Walters for a long time, based on the degree of her hair growth and bruising. The body of Ricky Lee Jones was found on March 3, 1991, in Lamar County, Mississippi. He was not identified until July of 2008. In the early morning of April 1, 1990, Officer Mike Miller of the Arizona Highway Patrol found a truck on the side of I-10 with its hazard lights on. When he investigated inside the cab, he discovered a nude woman, handcuffed and screaming.

The Storyteller Collection

There was also a male present, who identified himself as the driver of the truck. After failing to talk his way out of the situation, Rhoades was arrested and later charged with aggravated assault, sexual assault, and unlawful imprisonment. After further investigation, the arresting detective, Rick Barnhart, was able to make a connection to the Houston case and noticed a pattern stretching over the course of at least five months. In executing a search warrant of Rhoades' home, police found photos of a nude teenager, who was later identified as Walters; her body was found in September of 1990. Also present were photos of another female (Walsh), whose body was discovered that October.

In 1994, Rhoades was convicted of the first-degree murder of Regina Kay Walters and was sentenced to life without parole in Menard Correctional Center in Chester, IL. He was extradited to Utah in 2005 to be tried for the deaths of Candace Walsh and Douglas Zyskowski; however, per the victims' families' requests, the charges were dropped in 2006, and he was returned to prison. Rhoades later pleaded guilty to those crimes as well.

News Story #2

In 1978, Singleton raped fifteen-year-old Mary Vincent, cut off her forearms, and left her naked in a ditch near Modesto to die. In a decision that caused a furor in California, he was paroled in 1987 after serving eight years of a fourteen-year term. Outraged California communities refused to accept him, and authorities ended up housing him in a mobile home at San Quentin State Prison until his parole was up in 1988.

Singleton eventually moved to Tampa, where he had spent his childhood. Residents protested, and a car dealer offered him $5,000 to leave the state. A homemade bomb was detonated near the Singleton home, but nobody was injured. A jury in Florida convicted Singleton of murder for stabbing to death Roxanne Hayes, thirty-one, at his Tampa home in 1997. Vincent testified during Singleton's penalty hearing in Florida, pointing him out with an artificial limb. The retired merchant marine seaman denied raping and mutilating Vincent but admitted stabbing Hayes. "I'm sorry about the death in this case," he told the judge as he was sentenced to die. "I'll have to carry it on my conscience the rest of my life."

The Storyteller Collection

MarBrowders' The Storyteller©

The Call

The Storyteller Collection

The Storyteller Collection

The Call

In my distress I called upon the LORD, *and cried to my God: and he did hear my voice out of his temple, and my cry did enter into his ears.* —2 Samuel 22

It was late—very late—but he couldn't sleep. He had worked hard all day, trying to score without funds, and now that he had them, he was back in his little room, shaking with excitement that he had finally scored. He had acquired about an ounce of crack cocaine. This should take him where he needed to go for at least a day.

He didn't want to think about what he had to do to obtain it. It had come down to this; he was a man selling his body, for that was all he had left, all he still owned.

He had no more dignity and no more value. He was like so many others, just a strung-out junkie, living to get to his next fix. This was the first time he had only his body to sell. He had sold everything of value he had once owned, and now, his body was his only commodity. He chuckled a bit; he used to be worth so much more…

He had once been a valued employee in charge of new business procurement. He had worn suits and traveled around the country on behalf of his company, for which he had worked for eight years.

The Storyteller Collection

He had married the love of his life straight out of college—yes, he even had a college degree—and they had two twin daughters, who would turn six this year. He and his wife had bought a nice home and were planning on raising their family there.

They also had two cars and a boat. His income had afforded him to put his daughters in private school, and he had already tucked away their college tuitions. He began to think back that, prior to all this happening, he and his wife had talked of having another child...

He began to hunt for the pipe he used to heat up his drugs and found it. He dropped the crystal rock in it and began to twirl it over an open flame. He couldn't wait for it to vaporize; it would send him into a world of not thinking about the past. But before it did, his mind landed on how all this started—the beginning of his end. He had been in Virginia, concluding yet another successful deal for new business with a client he didn't know well. They had been sitting in a supper club, and the client had offered him a drink. He politely declined, stating that he was a Christian man and did not believe in drinking. He could see that the client's curiosity was piqued.

"So, you have no vices?" the client challenged him.

"By 'vices,' if you mean alcohol, then no." He smiled at the client, trying to keep things light.

"I don't know if I could trust a man without any human vices," countered the client. "Have you even ever tried a bit of blow?"

"No. What is 'blow'?" queried the man.
"Oh, something that clears your head," the client lied. He then pulled out white powder in a small baggie and poured some on the table of their booth. He then divided it into three lines and offered the man a straw-like tube to try it.

"I don't think so." The man backed away a little.
"Come on; it won't hurt you. Just try it once—just so you can say that you've experienced it."

The man, without knowing anything about narcotics, knew that this was a bad idea. But he had been down here a whole week, trying to conclude this business. He was one signature away. If one little line could seal this deal, he would do it. He didn't believe that one line would be detrimental to him.

The white powder sliced up his nose quickly. At first, it felt like a brain freeze, the kind that happens when one takes in too much cold soda. He shook his head to get rid of that feeling. The client just chuckled at him and sucked up the next two lines for himself.

The Storyteller Collection

As the man sat back, the brain freeze was being replaced with a euphoric feeling akin to great sex.

The pleasure center of his brain was wreaking havoc over his senses. What a rush of emotions! It was like nothing he had ever experienced. So this was what doing drugs felt like.

He noticed that his mind was clear, and he felt that his judgment wasn't impaired at all—or so he thought.

He felt energetic and had a strong sense of self-importance. And what did the client tell him—that it was not habit-forming? He knew that a few people at his place of employment indulged every now and then, and now he knew why.

The man concluded his business with the client the next day and headed back home. For some unknown reason, he kept thinking about the white powder his client called "cocaine" that he had tried. He was back to his old self now, and that high (for lack of a better word) was gone.

He had felt so alive and so sure of himself after he tried it. He felt that he could acquire new business from the masses. How could something so invigorating be so wrong?

The Storyteller Collection

Over the next few weeks, as he went about the activities of daily living, he found himself thinking about the cocaine. He wondered how one could obtain it, since it was not sold legally. One day, he found himself approaching one of the guys he knew who used it recreationally.

"Hey, I was wondering if you knew how to get some of that cocaine?" the man whispered in his ear. He could tell that his colleague was shocked.

"I thought you were a Christian," his colleague said. "That's why we never asked you to hang out with us."

"I am a Christian," retorted the man. "I tried it once on a business trip and was curious about it. That's all."

"Whatever, man," his colleague said. "We are all going over to the house of a friend of mine tonight. The blow will be flowing, but you had better bring some cash, because it's not cheap."

The man nodded that he would, and his colleague wrote down the address for him. The man was so excited about trying it again that it was all he thought of for the rest of the day.

He stopped off at an ATM and pulled out his limit: $500. He didn't know how much it would cost, but he felt that this should be enough.

The Storyteller Collection

He told his wife that he was meeting a client for dinner and a late meeting. He wondered why he felt the need to lie.

He began to feel that this was his adventure, all for himself, and he did not want to share it with her.

He made it to the address twenty minutes earlier than he should have.

He just waited in his car until he saw his colleagues pull up. He hands were shaking because he was so excited about this.

"You seem to have it bad," his colleague said to him, shaking his head as he saw him approach. "You had better be careful. Some people can use this for a lifetime and be okay. But there are some who try it one time and become hopelessly addicted."

"I did bring some money, like you said, but I don't know how much it costs." The words "hopelessly addicted" did not even penetrate his brain; as his client had told him, it was not addictive at all.

"How much money did you bring?" queried his colleague.

"Five hundred dollars."

"I guess you are serious about getting this party started."

He came back to the present; the smoke from the pipe encircling him now. His eyes lit up as he began to inhale the byproduct of his purchase. He remembered how the drugs used to make him feel: euphoric, energetic, smart, and courageous. Now, he needed it just to bring himself back to some semblance of normal—whatever that meant now.
In the beginning, with it all being so exciting, he couldn't wait to get to a cocaine party. While everyone snorted a bit and milled around while drinking cocktails, he only did cocaine, as he still considered himself a Christian, which meant that he did not drink.

It was now a little over a year later. He realized he had gone through their entire savings account of $130,000!

He didn't even remember taking it all out. What he did notice was that his drugs were consistently becoming more expensive. The first five hundred dollars went in that first night. It then became fifteen hundred dollars here, and five thousand dollars there, but he had no idea that he had depleted his entire savings.

This was getting way too expensive for him. It was time to stop, but he didn't. He cashed in some stocks and bonds, and finally, he tapped into his children's college funds.

The Storyteller Collection

He and his wife had been so proud to know that their children's future educational needs were secure. He would think every once in a while of what his wife would say if she found out, but his mind wasn't on the consequences, only the here and now.

By the second year, after his first drug odyssey, his boss fired him, as he was now using the company credit card for his personal use.

He had needed some money quickly one day, and all he had that wasn't maxed out was his corporate credit card. He thought that he would put the money back by his next payday; however, of course, just about all his paycheck went to his habit, and he never had the money available to put it back.

He had been fired; what was he going to do now? How could he afford his habit?

He languished around the house for a few days, not even thinking about searching for employment. He was trying to figure out where he would get the money to score.

Over the previous week, he had managed to sidestep the questions from his wife about his termination. He just vaguely said something about downsizing.

She was now wondering this: if that were true, where was his severance package?

The Storyteller Collection

The man's mind wasn't on being accountable to his wife; he was thinking of how he was going to pay for his next fix. Ah, he had it! He pulled the mortgage

papers out to assess what their house was worth. He had long since sold the boat and his own car, telling his wife that it had been recalled. That was one of stupidest lies he had told to date.

They had a fifteen-year mortgage; they had wanted to be debt-free by the time he reached fifty and had hoped that an early retirement would be on their horizon.

He had approximately $200,000 in equity in the house. That would tide them over until he secured new employment. But the next month, that line of equity was gone, too.

He was no longer shaking now. He was calmer and more in control of himself. He leaned back in his hotel bed, knowing he would be thrown out of there within a few days as well. He thought of the time when everything finally had hit the fan at home.

* * *

His wife had received a bounced check from their children's private school. She had said that it couldn't be right. She noticed first that they were overdrawn; she had gone to transfer money from their savings to their checking to cover it and found that they no longer had any money in their savings. But that was absurd—they had almost $140,000 in there.

The Storyteller Collection

She went home to speak to her husband, but he was nowhere in sight. For months now, he would just disappear, sometimes for hours, sometimes for days. He never had a rational reason for it, but she just let it slide.

She began to investigate their whole financial portfolio, and she could not believe what she saw. It was gone, all gone!

Their entire savings—annuities, stocks, and bonds—was gone. She began to shake as she checked their girls' college funds...yes, that money was gone, too. She had begun to shake her head in disbelief when she noticed an official letter from the mortgage company. Good lord, the line of equity her husband had taken out was gone, too! She thought, "What is going on here?"

He didn't know what to say to her. She was yelling and screaming at him, and all he could think of was what he could sell to get his next fix. He knew that she had every right to be angry, but he always felt that he would get another job and put it all back. The problem was that he was in no condition to find employment.

His wife kicked him out of the house. He knew he deserved it. He went from his parents' home to a little apartment, then quickly to a rat-infested hotel room that was paid for by the week. His parents were paying for that, as they would not allow him back in their home; he had begun to pawn some of their items for his fixes.

The Storyteller Collection

He took another hit off his pipe and began to think how he had obtained today's score. He was a man, and he was not gay, but his body was the only thing he had left to sell. It had been demoralizing to sell himself for a fix, but that's what it had come down to.

It was almost gone. What could he do now? He rarely ate; he didn't want to waste any money on food when he could use it for drugs. He realized now that he was skin and bones, a mere shadow of his former self. He was worth less than nothing. He remembered how he had to beg the dealer to use his body in exchange for drugs. The only thrill he believed the dealer had gotten out of it was the knowledge that he was not homosexual. It was late, very late. After today, he had finally decided to take his life.

He had reduced himself to nothing but a commodity and not a good one, at that. This was his last score, his last high, his last hurrah. His plan was to take his life before the dawn of a new day. It was as simple as that.

He was just about finished smoking the remains of his crack cocaine when a thought entered his head. He used to be a Christian. He used to believe in Jesus and follow His teachings. He used to mentor young men and remind them of Jesus' promise that He was the way, the truth, and the life.

He knew that Jesus would never leave, no matter how bad things got.

The Storyteller Collection

In his high stupor, the man decided to call Jesus. Just before he took his own life, he wanted to ask Jesus about those promises. His fingers were shaky as he made the call.

He knew it was late, but he was running out of time. He'd be dead by morning. He just wanted to talk to the Savior.

The phone rang only once, and he found an uplifting voice on the other end.

"Greetings, in the name of Jesus Christ," the voice on the phone said.

"He-hello?" The man hesitated.

"Hello," said the voice on the phone, with such compassion.

"I was wondering if I could speak to the Savior." He was unsure now why he had called.

"Certainly. He has been waiting for your call!" exclaimed the voice on the phone. "Please let me get Him for you."

"Well, maybe...after giving it some thought...I'll try Him later. I know He must be busy with others who are more important than me."

"You are just as important as all His children—even more now that you have called upon Him."

"Well," the man stammered, coming off his high, "frankly, I don't know what to say to Him now."
"Didn't you have a question for Him?" queried the voice on the phone.
"Yes, but now, I don't know how to ask it." The man was filled with trepidation. He had done so much wrong. He had lied, cheated, and stolen; what could he say to Him?

"Well, try it out on me," suggested the voice on the phone.

"Well...I..." stammered the man. "I will be dead by morning, but I just wanted to know if...if He remembered His promises."

"Trust me when I say that He remembers," the voice on the phone assured him.

"I...I know that his promises can't be for the likes of me.

But I was just thinking that I wanted to ask Him if His promises could be for a man like me?" The man was shaking all over.

"His promises were especially for someone like you," the voice on the phone said. "Someone who made a wrong turn in life, and lost his way.

He is excited to speak to you. As I said before, He was hoping that you would call."

The Storyteller Collection

"But how could He be glad to speak to the likes of me?" The man became angry. "I don't think He has any idea of what I have done.

"He blessed me with a college degree, a loving wife, and two children. He went on to bless me with a great job and comfortable finances to ensure that my life would be perfect.

I was a deacon in my church of worship, and I started a Big Brothers program so that boys without dads would have solid male role models to keep them on the straight and narrow.

"I had everything, but with one line of cocaine, I lost it all: my job, my wife and children, my finances, and even my home. I lied to my wife, and I stole from my parents and my place of employment. How could He even want to look at me, let alone hear my voice? No, this was a bad idea. I wouldn't know what to say to Him."

The man started to hang up, but the voice on the phone pleaded with him to listen.

"Please wait. Don't hang up. I speak the truth when I say that He has forgotten you not. He loves you and wants to restore what Satan has taken from you. Remember, Satan comes to steal kill and destroy.

But Jesus came that you would have more life and abundantly so. Do you think Jesus built up your wealth to such an extreme so quickly? He could have, but He did not.

"Satan pulled that evil trick on you. Remember that he once offered Jesus much if He would worship him. But Jesus saw him for what he was and said, 'Satan, get thee hence behind me,' and Satan fled. When you shut him out of your front door, he will slither around to a window.
Satan knew you would not drink, so he tempted you with something you knew little about.

"He then began to strip you of all your perceived wealth he had let you accumulate so quickly to reduce you to nothing. He then brought about the ultimate sin your eyes: he had you sell your body for drugs. A man of strong convictions was now little more than a prostitute. Now, Satan is waiting for you to commit suicide. He would then have you for eternity.

"But Jesus was sure you would call upon Him. He waited to hear from you so that He could help."

"You mean he knows about..." The man took a big gulp, his eyes bright. "About...that? I was never going to mention that to a soul. That was my last straw. How could I speak to Him, now that He knows what I did?"

"Do you have a minute while I tell you my story?" the voice on the phone asked. "You would still have time to kill yourself by dawn."

"Your story?" asked the man. "I...I'm sorry, but I just assumed that you were an operator."

The Storyteller Collection

"We all work Jesus' direct line for Him. It is an honor for us to do it. Our goal is not to let one soul disconnect before he or she can reach the Father. But let me tell you my story.

"Let me first introduce myself; I am Jabez."
"Jabez? I know of you! In Chronicles, in the listing of the lineage of the kings, there you were. You popped up out of nowhere."

"Yes, that's me; back then, I had several brothers. What I did not know at the time was that the Lord found me more honorable than my brothers. All my life, I had felt unworthy. My mother named me 'Jabez,' she said, because she bore me out of pain. Now, just imagine that each time someone says your name; it reminds you of all the pain your mother endured to give birth to you. I felt like a marked man with no worth, no hope, and no future.

"One day, I had reached the end of my rope, so I made the same call then that you made today. I asked the Lord if He would bless me—bless me, indeed, and enlarge my territory. I asked that He lay His hands on me and that He would keep me from evil so that I would not cause pain anymore to anyone in my life."

"Now I know this was a bold call but I had nothing to lose and everything to gain. As I listened intently on the line for his answer, I was overjoyed when he granted my request."

"I am telling you my story because it too all started with a call to him. I was at my wits end.

The Storyteller Collection

If I hadn't called on him who knows, I would probably have been contemplating what you are doing also."
"I implore you to speak to the Lord. Let me get him on the line. If he could change my life, surely he could change yours. Will you wait?"

Was it a coincidence that it was Jabez who picked up the line when he called? Someone else who had to make the same call once as he? Someone whose life was in a horrible state back then. He made the call and received Jesus' assurance. Tears began to slide down the man's face as he said, "I'll wait for I need to talk him so much."

As he waited for the Father to come on the line, he thought, I so need to hear the voice of the Lord...
The man soon heard a strong and yet compassionate voice come on the line. It was sweet, assured and kind. The man began to cry even harder as he hears the Father's voice. With a lump in his throat and crackle in his voice, he said, "Father, I need you!"

And the man heard the Father say, "I know, Son; I know."
End

Jesus said, "I am the way and the truth and the life. No one comes to the Father except through me."
John 14:6

The Storyteller Collection

The Storyteller Collection

The Storyteller Collection

The Murdered

Submit yourselves therefore to God. Resist the devil, and he will flee from you.

James 4:7

Her gait was unsure as they shuffled her into the courtroom. The shackles that bound her hands and feet clanked like old cowbells. The jail cell they had been keeping her in was dark and almost cave-like. She blinked repetitively, adjusting her eyes to the glaring light of the courtroom.

The bailiffs hurried her along, but the heaviness of the chains impeded her from moving as fast as they wanted her to. One thing that immediately caught her eye was the fact that the courtroom was filled to capacity. You'd think she was a celebrity and that this was the trial of the century, but she was no one special.

She was just a woman who had tried to live her life as best she could. She had worked down on Main Street at a job of little to no consequence. She had been there for twelve years now. She belonged to the local church, where she paid her tithe.

The Storyteller Collection

Her only true joys in life were reading her Bible and praying. She would read it whenever her free time permitted. Through the years, she had always felt that she was too inconsequential for the likes of Jesus ever to pay her any attention, but she did like to read about Him and get to know Him in this way.

She stayed mostly to herself. She caused no distress or harm to anyone; she was just a Ms. Nobody.

But one moment of rage and anger had changed all that forever. She was now on trial for her very life, and people came from near and far, especially from back in the pages of time.

One of the first things she noticed was the jury. There were twelve individuals, eagerly waiting to judge her. There were some she recognized; Pontius Pilate was there, waiting to judge her.

She remembered that his wife had had a dream of an innocent man, and, when Pontius Pilate had heard it, he had washed his hands of the whole mess by putting Jesus to death. She wondered how he would judge when his "yes" wasn't "yes" and his "no" wasn't "no."

Herodias sat there smugly. clinging her bracelets and rings together, whispering, "Off with her head!"

She once had her daughter dance for King Herod. It had delighted him so much so that he offered her daughter anything, up to half his kingdom. When she asked her mother, Herodias, what should she ask for, of course she had said, "The head of John the Baptist." The woman thought, "And she is to judge me?"

But she smiled when she saw Lydia, who was a seller of purple goods and was known as the first businesswoman. When she became baptized, she had made sure her whole household was, too. She was a faithful woman.

She was relieved to see her sitting there. And then there was Simon Peter. He was one of the original disciples. Even though he had denied Christ thrice on that fateful night, he did ask for forgiveness, and he went on to be a great leader, bringing many people to Christ. It seemed that there was a complete mixture in the jury box.

She didn't know how this would play out, but she would not lie. She had done it; she was guilty in that sense, but she felt that she was justified. It was justifiable homicide, not murder.

The apostle Paul was her attorney, and she was relieved. He was well aware of transformations, for he had transformed himself. Jesus had even changed his name.

He patted the back of her hand, whispering, "It will be all right," but as she looked at the prosecutor, she shivered—for there was Pharaoh.

He was the same pharaoh who had sanctioned the deaths of many babies in the hope that one of them would have been Moses. How was she to get any type of justice with the likes of him?

Her eyes turned to the judge as the court came to order. It was Moses! But, of course, it could be no other. He had been given the first laws. Who was better to judge? However, she shrank back, thinking, "He truly knows the law—all of it."

"I will hear opening statements now," Moses said. Pharaoh rose, as a king would, and said, "The facts of this case are clear. A fortnight ago, this woman did viciously and with malice cause the death of our supreme, benevolent, and generous benefactor: Satan."

There was grumbling suddenly in the court at the very mention of his name. Pharaoh looked around, nodding in agreement. "We also have witnesses to what happened that night, and we have the murder weapon. She cannot lie her way out of her despicable deed. Everyone knows of the night in question. She stated that the victim was trying to lure her into hell once again. And what did she do? She turned on him and murdered him and sent him straight to hell instead.

The Storyteller Collection

I'm here to show the facts of the case and why she should be found guilty and be put to death."

"Apostle Paul." Moses gave him the platform.

"Thank you, Moses." Paul stood and said, "My client is not a liar. She has admitted her part in all of this. However, based on the facts, it was justifiable homicide—"

"Justifiable homicide?" Pharaoh jumped up and yelled aloud, "There was no justification here. She murdered, and she must be punished!"

There was a roar in the gallery, and Moses pounded his gavel, trying to restore some semblance of order. "Pharaoh, you will get your chance to bring your witnesses forth. In the meantime, Paul has the floor."

"Your Honor," Paul said, "everyone has his or her breaking point, and she is no exception. She came into this world with dreams and goals and a bright future, as with all of us. She was God's beloved child. But Satan took a special interest in her, just because of who she was. In every area of her life, he caused destruction, disaster, and tragedy.

"At the end, he finally decided that he would have her commit suicide, the ultimate ending to one's life. She murdered him to save her own life.

The Storyteller Collection

I believe," Paul continued, "that, once all the evidence is in, my client will be found not guilty."

Paul reseated himself with dignity, patting his client's hand once again, letting her know that he had this.

"This was not going to turn out as Paul thinks," she thought. So many were angry over what she had done. Why had she gone so far? What was it that made had her say, "Enough is enough!"? Jesus had taught that "if any man sues you and takes away your coat, you should let him have your cloak also" (Matt. 5:40–41).

He had said that, if someone compels you to go a mile with them, you should go two. So why didn't she just take more from Satan and turn the other cheek? Now, she had broken one of the commandments: "Thou shalt not kill."

Hearing Moses speak again brought her back to the present. "We will hear the evidence against her, and then we will let the jury decide."

"I object, Your Honor; I object!" Pharaoh stated, "You know for a fact that it wasn't Satan's time to go. God said that he would be here during the Revelation, and she killed him prematurely and trapped him in hell before his time. Not only do we want her put to death but we also want Satan released."

The crowds seem to go wild, both for and against her.

Moses said, "We will not turn this into a sideshow. Pharaoh, call your first witness."

Pharaoh called a slimy little devil who was part of a legion, and he took the stand. "Do you promise to tell the truth—"

"There's no need for that; you know the truth isn't in him." Moses stated a fact. "He will never tell the whole truth. We will have to discern it from what he says."

The slimy, little devil, who was also known as part of the legion, just snickered.

"Well, what is your take on what happened that night?"

"Well, Your Honor," he said, "we were doing what we normally do—you know, getting people to drink, smoke, fornicate, murder each other… you know, just the norm. Well, Satan decided to go and see what she was up to, you know, for a kick—which was our right, Moses, which was our right! He found her on her knees, praying. Well, Satan had put a lot of time in on her, so he was beside himself to find her on her knees, talking to Jesus.

"He said to her, 'Why are you praying? Didn't I tell you that He doesn't love you?

He would never be there for you, you stupid woman. Don't you know it's over? You lost it all. I took your mother; I took your father. I strung your brother out on drugs and killed your child. I even had you gang-raped. And did Jesus show up? No! That's because He doesn't care for you. He is an absentee dad! Why hang on to the little remnant you call life? I've got some nice liquid poison here, just for you.'

"She said, 'I must pray, because only God knows why all these things have occurred to me. I must tell Him, I must let Him know that I still believe in Him—'

"Then, he said, 'You are as crazy as I thought you were.' But she continued to pray, and Satan continued to harass her without relent. He continued to recount her life and how bad it was and how the one she prayed to never came to her aid. Satan sat the poison on an end table by her and said, 'This is getting boring. Kill yourself, and be done with it. I told you that He doesn't care for you; look at what He allowed me to do to you.'

"Finally, she could not take his harassment any longer, and she began to cry. 'But He does love me. He just has to love me; He promised that He would never leave me and that He would be with me always.'"

"Satan said, 'He's left you here alone to deal with the likes of me. What Father who loved His child would do that? He doesn't love you; He just wants you out of His life.'

'No!' she screamed, 'I believe He loves me. He promised that He would restore all that was taken. He just has to love me! He said He would be there.'

"Then, Satan said, 'Well, is He here?' Satan kept badgering her all night long, saying over and over again that Jesus didn't care about her. Frankly, we all thought it was comical. We were taking bets as to the exact time she would kill herself.

"Stop it!" she screamed, 'I can't take it anymore!' And she turned around, and she murdered him!

"Well, Moses, I could hardly believe it. Satan, my lord and master—gone? Sent back to hell? It was unreal. I didn't trust her, so I ran out before she could kill me. I went to the authorities, and they came and arrested her for murder."

Pharaoh said, "That will do. The witness is all yours."

Paul nodded and said, "Thank you." He approached this devil, who was a part of a legion. "Are you a liar?" Paul accused him.

"Well, uh, this ain't about me. This is about what she did."

"I asked if you were a liar!"

"Well, okay. I've been known to tell a tale or two."

"You couldn't even be sworn in because your character is in such dispute," said Paul.

"Well, I know what I am, but this does not negate the fact that she murdered Satan."

"And what did he do to her?" Paul countered.

"He was just having a conversation with her. He never touched her, that's for sure. I'm telling the truth about that; he never touched her."

"Once again, you're lying. He did, in fact, 'touch' her. He touched her spirit, he touched her life, he touched her dreams, he touched her hopes, and he touched her family and friends."

"Well…um…" That devil began to stammer. "I stand on the Fifth."

"You can't stand on the Fifth; you're giving testimony. This isn't about you, not yet. No further questions, Moses."

The Storyteller Collection

Satan's sleazy devil slithered away like the raspy coward he was. "Call your next witness."

And Pharaoh called Gomer. Gomer smiled daintily as she proceeded up to the stand, winking at one of the bailiffs.

"Gomer, wife of Hosea?"
"Yes, Pharaoh."
"Now, you're married to a good man, a noble, Christian man. How does that work out for you?
"Not too well," she admitted. "He is always trying to get me to do the right things."

"So, you weren't home with your husband that night?"
"No, Sire."
"Well, where were you?"
"Well, I had a date—"
"A date?"

"Yeah. I was in the company of Satan."
"You were in the company of Satan?" echoed Pharaoh. "So, you were there also that night when the murder occurred?"

"Yes, I was," Gomer said smoothly.
"Tell me what you saw."

"Satan was—well, just being Satan, you know. He was just fooling around. We were just having some fun with her. We've teased her before. She never reacted like this.

It was kind of comical how she would react sometimes.

"She would cry like a little baby sometimes, and she would act all lost and stuffy at other times. Well, this time, she was on her knees, doing that prayer thing, and Satan was just having a conversation with her."

"Well, what did he say?"
"Oh, Satan was just being—well, Satan." She winked at Pharaoh. "He just taunted her a bit, telling her how God didn't love her and that she might as well go on and kill herself. But that's not the first time he had said that to her. She didn't go all crazy on him before."

"Mmm," Pharaoh pondered.
"But Satan was joking, and I was laughing."
"I see. And then what happened?"

"After a few hours, she became angry, and she rose up with a kind of fire in her belly. She let him have it, and he was dead. She sent him to hell. And what are we supposed to do without him? It was boring around here, and he made it fun and lively. Now, he's gone before his time. I think she should be boiled in oil."

From the jury box, Herodias said, "No! Cut off her head!"

The Storyteller Collection

Gomer started laughing, for she knew Herodias was fond of decapitation.

"Your witness, Paul."

Paul got up and said, "Gomer, you were out awfully late with someone who was not your husband."

"My husband is kind of a stick-in-the-mud, but we have this understanding."

"You have an understanding with your husband that you're to hang out with the likes of Satan? And your husband would approve? How many children do you have?"

"Oh, I don't know," she lied.

"Well, let me change the question. How many of your children belong to your husband?"

"Moses, can I object?" Gomer asked. "I'm not on trial here."

Moses said, "But your character is."

"Isn't it true that you've known many men and that at one time, you were put on the slavery block, and your husband had to purchase your freedom?"

"Well, so what if he did? He was my husband, you know." She crossed her arms in defiance.

"Your character is so questionable. How can anyone believe what you say?"

"Well, Satan ain't here, is he?" she countered. "He's back in hell, isn't he? I may be an adulterer, and I may be a tramp, but the facts are the facts."

"No more questions. I am through with this witness."

The woman began to sweat. There was so much evidence against her. She hadn't known they were even there in the room.
"Pharaoh, do you have any more witnesses?" Moses asked.

"No, Your Honor. The defense rests." He was so smug that she couldn't stand it.
"Paul, are you ready?"

"Yes, Moses. I call the defendant to the stand."
There were gasps and whooshes in the gallery as her chains were removed, and she took the stand.
"Do you swear to tell the truth and the whole truth?"

"Yes, I do," she stated honestly.
"So, let's go back to that night a fortnight ago. You were home, minding your own business?"
"Yes."

"Did you invite Satan in?"
"No." She shook her head.

"I never would have invited him in. I was praying in the hopes that Jesus would come, because I had something I wanted to tell Him."

"And what was that?"

"I—I just wanted to tell Him that, no matter what had happened to me in life, I still loved Him, and I still believed in Him."

"And then what happened?"

"Satan appeared instead, and once again, he started taunting me."

"So, Satan has done this before?"

"Yes. Normally, I just resist him, and he flees. But I was beseeching Jesus, so I just tried to ignore him."

"You know that, in order to get him to leave, you can't just ignore him. You have to resist Satan, and then he will flee."

"I understand that, but I wasn't focused on him at the time. So many terrible things have happened in my life, and I had lost my direction for a time. I just wanted Jesus to know that no matter what, I loved Him, and I wasn't going to try to understand His will anymore; I was just going to seek Him out in everything I do.

"Satan came uninvited, and he continued to rehash all that he done to me and tell me how Jesus never came to my assistance.

He brought up how he had taken my parents when I was but a teenager, who had left me without true direction, and I made a lot of mistakes because of it. He made a drug addict out of my oldest brother, who never recovered.

My beloved brother was finally killed over a drug deal. They never caught his killer. He killed my second son—"

She choked up at the memory, even though it had been many years ago. "He turned my family into a bunch of strangers; he took my hopes and my dreams. And when it seemed that he had done his worst, he had me gang-raped. I was almost killed in that event.

The worst of it all was that he had made me doubt my Lord and Savior. He kept telling me that Jesus didn't love me and that He had given him permission to destroy my life."

"So, Satan harassed you with old memories, old pain, and old lies?"

"Yes," she conceded. "But one day, I was reading the Bible, and a verse popped out to me: 'God so loved the whole world that he sacrificed his one and only son. Whoever will believe in him would not perish but will have ever lasting life' (John 3:16).

"Since I was part of this whole world, I thought that He must be including me in this. I continued to read about Jesus. The world treated Him deplorably, even though He had done nothing but try to help them.

He healed the sick and raised the dead. He fed a multitude, but that wasn't enough.

"He saved their very souls, yet it still wasn't enough. They wanted His life. And for the love of mankind, He gladly gave it so that we could all live. I then found another scripture that told me not to worry; it said that, whatever had happened, he would restore what the palmerworm and the cankerworm the caterpillar had taken (Joel 2:25).

"He promised me that He would restore what was lost. So I prayed that night because I wanted to apologize to Him. I wanted Him to know that I still believed in Him."

"So, tell me what happened to Satan early that morning," Paul said.

"He was at me all night, until I couldn't take it anymore. I turned with the resolution of resisting him, and everything he had done to me came into focus. I screamed at him, and there was a white flash. When the light subsided, he was gone.

The Storyteller Collection

I guess his friends saw what I did, so I assumed it was so, but I don't remember."

"Oh, she has decided to use the 'Twinkie' defense," Pharaoh jeered.

"Silence!" Moses said.

"Have you told the truth here?" Paul looked into her eyes.

"Yes, I have."

"Your witness," Paul said to Pharaoh.

"So, the sun, the moon, and the stars got in your eyes, and that is why you can't remember exactly what you did?" Pharaoh was being facetious.

"I didn't say that."

"Well, I have exhibit A here, Moses: the Bible, God's Word. So you are telling this jury that you couldn't remember exactly what happened?"

"I—I turned and saw a bright light."

"When you got off your knees and stood, did you pick up this Bible?"

"I may have."
"You did. We have evidence of that. You hurled potent scriptures at him like knives, did you not?"
"I think I was speaking in tongues."

"Well, let's look up those tongued scriptures you hurled at him." Pharaoh began to flick through the Bible.

"Did you yell at him that he would become your footstool?"

"I don't remember."

"Did you say, 'I banish you in the name of Jesus'?"

Everyone began to gasp. They knew the power in Jesus' name.
"It could be possible, but I just remember a light."
"I rest my case."

Paul sat for a while and then looked up, as Moses asked, "Do you have any witnesses for your defense?"
"Moses, I have but one witness to call. He has traveled far, but He was determined to be here and to stand up for her. I found that there was another in that room a fortnight ago."

"I don't believe you, Paul," Pharaoh discounted him. "There were no other witnesses but the two I called."

"Just because He wasn't seen does not mean He wasn't there. I call Jesus Christ, our Lord and Savior, to the stand."

The Storyteller Collection

The courtroom erupted, as some of Satan's henchmen slithered out of the room. They were well aware of what Jesus did to the legion, and they didn't want to be a part of that annihilation again. He even made Pharaoh stutter.

"J-Jesus?" He could not believe his ears.

Jesus humbly but succinctly walked into the courtroom and took the stand.

"Father." Paul bowed. "Since you are the Word, there is no need for You to be sworn in. Saint and sinner alike know that You will not lie."

Jesus nodded at his respect and said, "The truth is the truth, and I cannot lie."

The woman looked up; she couldn't believe her eyes. Satan had said over and over again that Jesus didn't love her. Once again, Satan had lied. She was now glad that he was dead.
Her Lord and Savior did love her; He had come to speak on her behalf. He came just for her. Jesus smiled compassionately on the just and the unjust.

"My Father said a liar would not tarry in his sight."

"Jesus, were you there the night these things occurred?"

Jesus said, "Yes, I was there."
She looked at Jesus again. He had been there? But that night, she had felt so alone...
"What did you see, Savior?"

"I saw my daughter praying to me. I began stroking her hair, letting her know it was going to be all right and that I was there and I would always

be there. I would never leave her. While we were interacting, Satan flew in. He began to taunt her and reminded her of the years of her trials and tribulations. He failed to mention that, through it all, I was there, healing the wounds he had created.

"Where he took her back one step, I took her forward two. He just focused on the bad things in her life and did not remind her of all the good, such as the fact that I had given her more beautiful children. He didn't tell her that the one she had lost was with me and that her beginnings may have been humble, but her ending would be great.
"In the beginning, she wasn't educated, but now, she held a Ph.D. Satan will always embellish the negative and fail to admit all the positive. He failed to mention that, whatever happens, My promise assured that I would restore what would be lost.

"It didn't matter what the cankerworm or the palmerworm or the caterpillar and the locust did. I said that I would restore that which was lost.

"I had to stay close by her, for he was there to take her very life. I admit that she was confused that night, but I gave her a sword—the Word—with which to protect herself. And I had her put on her whole armor, and I was right there with my child.

"When she could take it no more, she ran to her desk pulled out her Bible. She opened it and started reading scripture after scripture, aimed straight at Satan's

heart. She rose up, pummeling him with the Word. You see, she didn't murder him,"

Everyone in the room gasped in unison, as she looked up at Jesus, confused; she thought she had murdered Satan. "He fled to hell like the coward he was," Jesus said.
Noise erupted. "My daughter never murdered him... she *convicted* him! And he committed suicide!
"Satan is one of my Father's fallen angels. He decided he wanted to be God himself, and it was God's word that put him in hell in the first place. She just took God's Word out and sent him back."

"There was no murder committed here; there was no justifiable homicide. There was recompense. There was retribution. But there was no murder."
"Thank you, Christ," Paul said.

Paul looked at Pharaoh. "Your witness."
"Jesus Christ." Venom slithered from Pharaoh's mouth. "Of course, You would show up at the eleventh hour, trying to save her.

The Storyteller Collection

This is just what You do. What makes You think that she is going to get off just by what You said?"

"I don't believe that she is going to get off just by what I've said, even though I told the truth. But if she is found guilty this day, I will die for her, because I promised her that I would be with her always, even to the ends of the earth. I would even die for her."

The woman looked up at her Lord and Savior and then realized that she had never been alone. She had never been out of his sight for one minute. The lies of Satan had kept her from seeing that her Lord was with her. He had said it so much that some part of her had begun to believe him.
But even in her faulty spirit, Jesus stayed with her and came to bear witness for her.

Jesus believed in her, and He believed in her innocence and was ready to die again so that she might continue to live.

Pharaoh had nothing more to say.
"Thank you, Jesus, for coming in and delivering the truth," Paul said.

As Jesus stepped down, he smiled so compassionately at His daughter that warm tears graced her eyes. They were tears of joy, full of the love she had for her Father. Jesus came down off the stand and stood by His daughter to let her know that He would always be there for her.

End

The Storyteller Collection

The Storyteller Collection

The Storyteller Collection

The Storyteller Collection

The Promise

Prologue

The front door closed unceremoniously behind her as she entered her well-appointed home. She removed her shoes in her little foyer and sat them neatly by an entrance table, where she discarded her keys and handbag, as was her normal ritual. Sighing a bit, she walked fully into her beautiful living room. She loved how tastefully she had set up her home. She felt that it was contemporary—like her.

Glancing at her watch as she walked across the room, she noticed that it was four o'clock in the morning. It wasn't unusual for her to get home at this hour, not for an escort. But she felt she was not just any type of escort; she considered herself to be "high-end." She was earning at least $5,000 per night.

She had worked smartly to get where she was. She had never walked the streets like common prostitutes—no, not her. She had been wise. She was a college graduate who had interviewed with a married man for a job. He had told that her she was too lovely and classy for a menial "nine to five" job. He propositioned her to travel with him to the Orient.

The Storyteller Collection

He had business there and said that he would love to have her on his arm as he traveled.

He had expressed to her that he would pay her well to do this and had quoted a $50,000 price for two weeks of her time! She couldn't believe the amount of money he was offering her for one trip.

It was during that trip that she came to realize that she would make more money as an escort than she would in a corporate position. At the end of the trip, the man was so pleased that he had recommended her to his friends, who also wanted some of her time—discreetly, as they were married, too. Within a year's time, she was quite a busy little lady. She planned smartly; she only worked three weeks out of a month and ten months out of a year.

She did not allow anyone to pay her bills; therefore, no one knew where she lived. She would have a "client" deposit the agreed-upon amount of money into her special account that was labeled Design Consultations. This was important to her, as she had family and friends who knew nothing of her occupation. She viewed the world of escorting like a business. She had been at it for five years now, and she surmised that she could retire completely in ten more years. She felt that she would still be young enough to get married and start a family.

The Storyteller Collection

As this contemporary woman crossed her living room and walked down a short hall, she entered into her well-detailed bedroom, decorated in sage and white. She mentally patted herself on the back for her fine taste. Her home was completely paid off; everything she owned was paid for, even her expensive sports car. She began to disrobe for bed, as her thoughts settled on her family.

Her parents had passed away when she was a child in a senseless home robbery that, according to the police, had gone terribly wrong. It happened when she was spending the night at her favorite aunt's house. For many years, her little mind felt that, if she had been there, she could have saved them. However, as she grew into her teen years, she blamed God for not saving them;

He had left her all alone, she felt, to fend for herself. With no brothers or sisters, she felt she had to become self-reliant. She asked little from her extended family as she grew up. She felt that all she needed was to grow up and get out on her own.

She had been taken in and raised by her favorite aunt, her father's sister, who was very religious. She remembered how her aunt had fought other members of the family for the opportunity to raise her, and she had won. The woman remembered how her aunt would tell other family members that she needed her.

Shaking her head in dismay, she didn't know where her aunt had come up with that one, but she had.

The contemporary woman felt that she had changed back then. She was no longer a happy-go-lucky child; she felt that she had to take care of herself. She had once heard a family member stating that whoever was going to get her would be paid well from her parents' social security and death benefits. She had just assumed that this was why everyone had wanted her, and her aunt won in the end.

The contemporary woman vowed that she would do everything she could to grow up quickly and leave. Before her parents died, she had felt loved by her aunt, but after their deaths, she felt suspicious of her. Truthfully, she felt suspicious of everyone.

As she slipped out of her designer pantsuit, she could still remember her aunt dragging her from one church function to another. Even back then, she promised herself that, when she was grown, she would be done with all that religious nonsense.

She could still hear the pastor shaking his fist, stating that Jesus died on the cross for our sins, and if the same circumstances arose today.

He would do it again because He loves us and because He made a promise to take away the sins of the world.

The woman smirked a bit, thinking, "Why would anyone want to go through all that again. Wasn't once enough?" She felt that, in today's world, people have to use their heads, not their emotions, to get ahead.

She slipped one of her favorite exquisite sleeping gowns on and sauntered to the bathroom. She had begun to wash her face and brush her teeth when her mind went to her aunt once again. She was in her seventies now, and she did not see her as often as she probably should, but if she felt affection for anyone, it would be her aunt.

Her aunt never had children of her own, so she had raised the woman with all the love and care she could. The contemporary woman had to admit that she was taken aback days before her high school graduation, when her aunt had presented her with a bank account with more than enough money for her to attend any four-year college of her choosing. Her aunt had saved up all the money she had received from the woman's parents so that she could obtain a sound education.

The contemporary woman's only gripe was that her aunt was constantly telling her to remember that Jesus made a promise to keep her safe.

The Storyteller Collection

She would say, "Honey, I pray for you day and night, and Jesus has promised me to watch out for you and keep you safe. He promised me that He would never leave you nor forsake you.

So don't worry. He will always have your back."
"But, Aunt," she would counter, "what if I don't want Him to have my back? I can take care of myself, you know."

"Oh, child." Her aunt shook her head. "It is thinking like this that makes me realize you need Him more than you know."

Rinsing her mouth out with mouthwash, she sighed as went into her bedroom and slid under the covers. She thought, "If my aunt could see my lifestyle now, she would have a coronary!" That is why she chose to live in a city, too far for family and friends to come without calling in advance.

She snuggled down in her soft bed, closing her eyes. Yes, she had left nothing in her life to chance. She was the epitome of today's contemporary woman.

* * *

She couldn't remember what she was dreaming of, but it must have been nice, because she was a bit angry for being awakened from it. What was it that woke her up? She listened for a few brief seconds and thought it was nothing.

She had turned over and repositioned herself on her pillow to sink back into sleep, when she heard something again...pounding? She sat up to listen once more.

There it was again—boards dropping, hammering, clanking...what the hell was going on?

Throwing back the covers of her bed, she threw her legs over the side and pushed her feet into her slippers. Before standing, she glanced at the clock and noticed that it was six o'clock in the morning! Goodness, she had only been asleep for two hours! Who would start any kind of construction at this hour?

She was now standing, grabbing for her robe and walking toward the window simultaneously. She pulled the curtains back to look. What was going on? There was a group of what appeared to be old men out there sawing and carrying lumber, while others were digging a hole—in her yard!

This was ludicrous! She would put a stop to this immediately. It was clear that they were at the wrong house. Though she was known to always be completely well-groomed when leaving her house, she didn't care that her hair was all over her head; she had, after all, been in bed, and normally, she didn't get up until eleven.

The Storyteller Collection

She exited her home, taking the steps two at a time until she was out in her front yard. Allowing a few seconds for her eyes to get accustomed to the early morning light, she glanced at these interlopers that were assaulting her well-manicured lawn.

"Is this some kind of joke?" was her first thought, as she noticed these weren't normal-looking construction workers; they were men in robes and turbans like back in the days of old—wait a minute! She appeared to recognize one of them from all the times she was in Sunday school. No...it couldn't be...Simon Peter? Oh my, it was Simon Peter! She then looked at the others. Why, there was Matthew, Thomas, and others: the disciples! She must be still asleep. What would the disciples be doing in her yard? Why were they digging a large hole?

"Excuse me," she said politely, shaking the cobwebs from her head. "Can you tell me what you're doing in my yard? I mean, is this some kind of practical joke?"

"No, my child." Thomas sighed, looking sad and forlorn. "There is no levity in this task. The Father made your aunt a promise, so He is coming."

"The Father? You mean Jesus Christ?" she asked. "Whatever for?" This was all so confusing for her. Why would Jesus come to her little abode?

Weren't there many more souls who needed Him now? "And for heaven's sake, stop digging that hole in my yard!"

Simon Peter stopped cutting the old, weathered wood and looked at her solemnly. "He is coming to climb back on the cross; this time, it is for your sins.

He made this promise many years ago to your aunt, so He is on his way." Clearly, Simon Peter had been crying. They all seemed to have been, as they went back to the task of cutting wood and erecting a cross, as requested by Jesus.

She was confused. She didn't need any help. She was fine. "Look, this is unnecessary, really. My aunt is in her seventies, and at times, she doesn't know what she is praying for. She has done this for years. Look. Can't you see that I am fine? I am healthy, happy, and whole. There is truly no need for…all this."

The disciples ignored her, turned, and continued their task. Simon Peter had concluded and was cutting the final piece needed. Matthew began layering the lumber together to make it thick, putting some type of glue between the layers, while John was tying it tightly with some kind of rope. Philip and Bartholomew were continuing to dig an enormous hole in the center of her yard.

The Storyteller Collection

Why, this was ludicrous!

She began to look past the construction, and she saw a woman. She was intertwining thorns into a kind of crown. She thought, "Maybe she will listen to me."

"Excuse me." The woman was polite in speaking to her. "What is your name?"

The woman bowed before her and said, "I am just a woman from Samaria. People know me as the only woman of my time to whom Jesus spoke."
"I have heard of you. You are the Samaritan woman by the well." The woman was referencing John 4:7–26.

"Tell me, how can I get them to stop all this madness? I have no wish to see Jesus go back up on the cross, but His disciples won't listen to me."
"Greetings, my daughter, in the name of our Lord and Savior, Jesus Christ." She bowed humbly before the young woman.

"Oh, honey. Times have changed since your time on this planet. Women don't have to act subserviently; this is a free country." The contemporary woman stated this with pride.

"I beg to differ," the Samaritan woman interjected.

The Storyteller Collection

"There are different kinds of bondages we are unaware of. And yes, you do need Him to once again climb up on the cross," the Samaritan woman said simply, continuing her appointed task of weaving the crown of thorns.

"Look, I'm about to lose my patience with all of you." The woman pulled her robe tighter about her body. "I neither want nor need Jesus' help. My life is fine; in fact, it is perfect. Do you see where I live? I'm a young woman, yet I own my own home and my own car.

I have more than $50,000 in the bank, attributed to the fact that I make in excess of $5,000 per day. My life could not be any better now if I tried to make it so. So tell me. What does Jesus think that His climbing back on that cross will do for me?"

Turning to the disciples once more, she shouted, "Stop that digging!"

The Samaritan woman stopped weaving the crown of thorns, as she sat on the short retaining wall outside of this woman's home. She gave her a sad smile and said, "You know, wise King Solomon once said that 'there is nothing new under the sun, and with each generation, I find no observance truer.'" She was referencing. Ecclesiastes 1:9 (NIV).

The Storyteller Collection

"I know this because you remind me of myself, back in my day. I, too, felt like I wanted to live my own life contrary to the laws and traditions of the time. I was what you would call today 'a contemporary woman.' I had no desire to become what was traditional at the time, which was a wife and mother. However, I was under the authority of my parents, as were all girls at that time until they were married off.

"Therefore, I did not marry for love; I initially married my first husband to gain my freedom from my parents' authority over me.
Once married, my first husband and I relocated to another town at my insistence, far away from family and friends. It was at that time that I obtained a bill of divorcement and left my first husband.

"I reveled in my freedom but soon realized that it was dangerous not to be under the covenant and protection of a man at the time, so I married my second husband, because he was like none I had ever known: exciting and dangerous. He, like me, was opposed to the norms of society of the day. We broke every rule in the book at the time. However, I left him for the same reason I married him: because he was dangerous. When he couldn't find others to exact his anger on, he would exact it on me.

"I then married my third husband for his wealth. My looks were still intact, and, since I had no children of my own, he was under the illusion that he was my first husband, and I did not alter his false impressions of me. Oh, child, life as a wealthy woman was a dream come true, and though I had no feelings for this husband, his wealth did keep me warm at night. Alas, tragedy struck, when he died of too much wine and too little care at my hand. I believed I would be a rich widow; however, his family learned of my past and found that I had no bill of divorcement from my second husband.

"Needless to say, I was left with nothing. I married my fourth husband out of desperation, as I was starving and he was convenient. He was much older than myself, but love wasn't on my agenda at the time, only survival. Once I was back on my feet, I found him wanting in the marriage bed, so I took a lover—my fifth husband. Knowing that I would be stoned if I were caught in my adultery, my fifth husband caused the demise of my fourth husband.

"I thought my life was now without a care in the world, as, finally, I was married to someone with whom I was in love. When my looks began to fade some years later, my fifth husband left me for a younger version of myself.

"When I met Jesus, I was living with a man who was not my husband. My looks were gone, and not only was I a Samaritan (a mixed-race people who were shunned by most), but no man wanted to marry me at this junction of my life. I was my lover's concubine, a status lower than a wife. Each day, I would pray not to anger him, lest he rid himself of me.

"Every day, I would go to the well to draw our daily water, secretly wishing that I was the coveted wife again of my first husband, as he was kind, decent, and good. But I never saw him as that;

I just saw him as a gateway to my freedom."

"Wow." The modern woman couldn't help being interested in the Samaritan woman's life story. She had known that she had had five husbands but did not know her life's journey through them, which ultimately led to her living with a man to whom she was not married. "I have to say that you have had a turbulent life. But my life is different; I have never been married. I am educated, and, more importantly, I have an exit strategy. Why, within the next five years, I plan—"

"Your plans?" scoffed the Samaritan. "You want to give God a good laugh? Tell Him what your plans are. There is no easy exit from the lives we choose to live; there are only consequences.

"Your plan is to make a lot of money, right? What happens along the way if your time is cut short because of something unforeseen? What if you have just enough time left to look over the remnants of your life? What then?"

"Well, I would..." said the woman. She thought, "Why is she hitting me with all these 'what ifs' unless she knows something I don't?"

"Daughter, you lost your parents at an early age, and since then, you have not wanted to cleave to anyone. Your aunt who raised you saw this in you. The more she loved you, the more you would pull away from her.

Your aunt is and has always been a God-fearing woman, so she prayed every day for your life.

"She beseeched Jesus on your behalf to save you, sanctify you, and fill you with His Holy Spirit. She exacted this promise from Him. But the more He would pour out love toward you, the more your heart would harden, because you felt like He took your parents away and left you alone. I am here to say that He did not leave you alone. He left you with family who loved and cared for you, family who pray for you, night and day.

"The acts you are committing are not condoned by Him, but He has still covered you with His grace. Now, your sins are heavy, and it seems that you embrace nothing He sends your way.

In order for you live, He must climb up on that cross once more.

"He has to get through to you that He loves you—no matter what. He is willing to do for you what He has not done for another, and that is to shed His blood a second time. Child, don't you see? That is how much He loves you! He is on His way to your country, your town, and your street. He has your address correct.

"The disciples never thought they would have to endure this again, but the Father stated that you were worth it. At His direction, the disciples were sent to build another cross that's exacted just for you. They are digging this hole in your yard to let you know that this is all about you and no other. The nails are set; the crown of thorns is just about completed. He made a promise to save your soul and to deliver you from the hands of the evil one. He made a covenant with your aunt that Satan could not have you, and if it takes Him climbing back up on that cross again, then so be it."

The woman was confused now. How did He know that she harbored anger in her heart toward Him for taking her parents away from her? She had never mentioned this to a soul. She looked again at the Samaritan woman, who lifted up the crown and started weaving it again. Her hands, she now noticed, were shaking; she, too, was upset to see

The Storyteller Collection

Jesus go through this once again. Wait a minute! He had told this woman of her past, too. Didn't He say to her that He knew that she had had five husbands and that the man she was living with was not her husband? He had told the Samaritan woman her life's story, just like the Samaritan woman was telling her hers.

"Can I ask you something, please?" the woman said to the Samaritan woman politely. She nodded. "Jesus did the same for you, didn't He? I mean, He didn't climb back on the cross, but He broke all the rules of the day for you."

"Yes, He did," admitted the Samaritan woman. "Just by asking me for a drink of water,

He broke a cardinal rule that day, but He felt that I was worth saving. I couldn't understand why He felt the need to speak to me directly and present Himself, but He did. I know now that, if He had done anything less, I, like you, would have scoffed at it. But He loved me enough to seek me out and talk to me more than any other woman in history. He deemed me worthy to share the knowledge of how to worship God, which was in spirit and in truth. He is doing the same for you now, as He had done for me. He is coming to show you how special you are to Him and that He is willing to die again, so that you might finally live."

The Storyteller Collection

The woman had no idea she had begun cry, but she had. All her life, she had thought that no one could truly love her but her parents, and since Jesus took them away, she refused to be loved by anyone else. She had shunned anyone who tried to show her love: her aunt, her two uncles, her cousins, and so forth.

The disciples were here at the direction of Jesus. This lovely Samaritan woman cared enough to explain Jesus's reason for this new sacrifice. It seemed that everyone was loving on her but herself. There were so many souls needing Him and praying for His presence, but He chose her, all because He loved her and had made a promise to her aunt.

"Oh Lord," she silently cried, "How can I stop this!" She didn't want Him to climb up on that cross. She wanted Him to know that she understood now and that there was no need for Him to make yet another sacrifice.

"Madam..." the young woman said softly, clearly affected by all of this. "I've done a great wrong against Jesus. H-how can I rectify this? I mean, I don't want to hurt Him again. What must I do?" The young woman was frantic.

"Just tell Him." The Samaritan woman smiled; relief creased across her face as she laid aside the unfinished crown.

The disciples overheard her plea and also stopped their tasks.

The woman fell on her knees, clutching her hands together, and said, "Father, I want to thank You for loving me enough to make such a great sacrifice. I want to thank You for Your grace over my life and for showing me the lengths You are willing to go just for me.

"I realize now that I am important to You and that You did not take my parents from me; You allowed someone else to experience the gift of parenting in their stead. Father, forgive me for the wrong I have done against You, as I humbly accept You as my Lord and Savior from this day forward."

Epilogue

The woman began to stir from her slumber, stretching contentedly as she slowly opened her eyes. It suddenly dawned on her that she was in her bed and didn't remember getting back into it after she spoke to the Samaritan woman and the disciples. "Had it all been a dream?" she thought, as she scooted up in the bed, putting her knees up to her chin and wrapping her arms around them.

Glancing over at her clock, she noted that it was nine o'clock in the morning. She touched her cheek and found that it was moist, as if she had been crying.

Pulling the covers back in haste, she scurried out of bed with a singular thought in mind and rushed to the window for a look. How could she explain all of this? There were no saws, lumber, nails, or holes in her yard. The disciples weren't there, and neither was the Samaritan woman. So—did she dream it all?

It couldn't have been a dream, for she felt different; she felt like a heavy burden had been lifted from her. She no longer felt angry over her parents' loss, as she had felt for so many years. In fact, she felt loved, wanted, and protected. She felt that it was time to love and respect the life with which she was blessed. But what could she do?

She wouldn't even allow her friends too closely into her inner circle. She felt that she would be self-sufficient and truly did not need or want love—well, until now. How should she start?
While she was trying to figure all this out, her phone rang. "Hello?" the woman said, as she pulled on her robe.

"Honey, it's me." She knew the sweet voice of her aunt. "Is everything all right there?"
"Oh, yes. I just had an amazing dream; I'm still trying to make heads or tails of it."

The Storyteller Collection

"You know, that's interesting. I had a dream as well. I dreamed that the Samaritan woman at the well came for a visit and told me that you would be moving home soon.

I just had to call you to find out if that were true."

Moving home? The Samaritan woman? Then, it wasn't a dream—it had all happened. And she had just been given her directed path.

"Yes, Auntie, I've decided to sell my house here and move home to you."

"Oh, praise God! Jesus has answered my prayers!" her aunt said gleefully. "I knew He would keep His promise to me!"

End

But the scripture hath concluded all under sin,
that the promise by faith of Jesus Christ might
be given to them that believe.
Galatians 3:22

The Storyteller Collection

The Storyteller Collection

The Storyteller Collection

Telling Lies

Wherefore putting away lying, speak every man truth with his neighbour:
for we are members one of another.
Ephesians 4:25

The pastor was sitting behind his desk, deep in thought. He had come a long way from that of a penniless struggling youth to a well-respected and revered pastor of a church the size of this one.

His congregation rivaled any that of televangelist out at the time; he had finally arrived. He viewed his pastoral calling like a business. He dealt with finances and balance sheets. He had more than one hundred employees on his payroll. He was no longer up and coming—he was there.

It had taken blood, sweat, and tears to get here, and, yes, he admitted, some lying and cheating as well. But if you want to go big, you have to sometimes fake it until you make it—and he had made it.

He felt no compulsion in lying; after all, he was sacrificing in the name of Jesus Christ. Jesus knew what it took to help His people in times like today.

The pastor was so deep in thought that the knock on the door occurred a second time before it got his attention. "Who is that?" he thought, irritated. He had no appointments at this hour. He glanced at his watch; it was 6:00 p.m. on a Sunday afternoon. Everyone should be gone and the sanctuary locked up. He had a dinner date in an hour with a young lady he had been seeing for more than a year now.

Whoever is at this door had better make it quick. He had to be home by 11:00 p.m., or his wife would question him...again.

"Come in." His baritone voice vibrated through the room, as the person silently entered. The pastor recognized the young man as someone in his congregation. He was the only son of Meredith and Joe.

"Hello, Pastor." The young man bowed his head slightly, giving respect, as one does to a man of the pastor's position.

"My, my," the pastor greeted him, "Each time I see you, you've grown more and more." The young man smiled humbly and nodded.

"I remember when I took over this church; you were about twelve, weren't you?" The young man nodded again, "And now look at you, a full-grown man. How old are you now? Thirty-five?"

"No, sir. I am thirty-three now," the young man corrected him.

"Thirty-three," the pastor repeated, leaning back in his swivel chair. "Time does fly by. Well, sit down, my boy, and tell me what's on your mind." The young man eased into the chair across the desk from the pastor. "I hope I am not bothering you, sir, but I have made some decisions in my life that I want to share with you. I have some questions, too."

"So, tell me what's on your mind?" The pastor was hoping he would be quick about it, as he had not seen his young lady for an entire week, and he didn't want to be late.

"I've decided on a career path for myself. I want to become an evangelist."

"An evangelist? Why an evangelist? Why not a pastor, like me?"

"I feel my true calling is evangelism. I truly want to get personal with people, you know, one-on-one. I feel I can be of better use in this capacity."
"Well, if you're looking for my blessing, you have it, Son."

"Thank you, Pastor. But I came to you because I have some reservations about my chosen vocation."

"So, tell me what concerns you, Son?" (*"And be quick about it,"* he thought. *"I have to leave in forty-five minutes."*)

"Well, Pastor, I need your help. I am struggling with the Ten Commandments. They have me perplexed in some areas."

"What specifically are you struggling with in the Ten Commandments?"

"'Thou shalt not bear false witness,'" said the young man.

"Telling lies? Well, let's take a quick look at it, and maybe I can help you clear it up." The pastor reached up on the shelf behind his desk and retrieved a smartly bound Bible, while the young man pulled from his pocket a small, black, weather-worn, nondescript Bible that had seen better days. It appeared to have been read so frequently that some of the pages had to be reshuffled inside.

"Okay, let's look at that particular commandment. The commandments can be found in..." The Pastor fanned the pages of the Bible.
"Exodus, sir. Chapter twenty, verse one," the young man interjected.

The pastor glanced up at the young man, "Yes. You seem to know your passages."

"I've been having some struggles with this; that's why I know it so well," explained the young man. "Pastor, I have thoroughly reviewed the Ten Commandments, because I wanted to make sure my heart was right before I embarked on this vocation in evangelism. Now, I get the first one, in which it says, 'Thou shalt not have any god before me.' I believe that I have a great understanding of this particular commandment. I would never put anyone or anything above God.

"And I've got the second commandment down, regarding false idols. I understand that idols include all images, be they of heavenly or earthly realms. I also understand that we are not to make our fellow man or beast higher than God is in our eyes. This commandment is secure in my heart.

"And in the third commandment, God says not to use His name in vain. Pastor, I love God so much, it would break my heart if I broke this commandment."

"Good, good, Son. Excellent." The pastor that felt the young man seemed to have a grasp on these earlier laws. "I can see you've studied and meditated on these things."

"Oh, yes, Pastor. I am determined to do a good job for God's people, even if I have to die to do it."

"Well, Son, that's a bit extreme, but I understand your level of conviction."

"Now, Pastor, I am comfortable with murder, too. I can't even envision myself taking a life that I can't replace. I am also good with keeping the Sabbath day holy. Pastor, in all the years since I began attending this the church, I have not missed one service you've preached. Remember, you once gave me a plaque for it some years back?"

"Yes, Son, you have really been a faithful and willing servant."

"And, Pastor, I don't relinquish my teachings after I leave church, because I carry them in my heart."

"Well fine, young man, fine. I have never seen anyone so diligent. You have certainly led by example here." The pastor smiled, looking at his watch again.

"Pastor, I love and respect my fellow man so much that I would not covet his wife or his possessions. I would not do that, Pastor. It's just not what I'm made of. I want to heal; I don't want to destroy."

"My son, you really seem to have God's law given to Moses at work deep down in your soul. So I don't see what your concern is?"

"But each time I get to 'thou shalt not bear false witness…'"

And the pastor said, "Yes, thou shalt not lie."
"When I get to this commandment, I feel… trepidation. You see, Pastor, people view telling lies as a game. They will re-label it and repackage it so that it doesn't look like what it is. People have re-branded lying by calling it 'misrepresenting.' They have colored lies to make them look more attractive—little white lies or pink lies…or levels of gray.

They think that when they lie out of omission, or if no one finds out about the lie, it is not a lie. Pastor, how does one get past telling these lies? I believe that people are ready and willing to refrain from everything else, but when it comes to lying, they feel they have an open-door policy."

"Well, I get what you're saying, Son."
The young man continued, "Lies have become so prevalent that people, at times, don't even realize they're lying. And, of course, lying is akin to cheating and stealing, because you are taking someone's faith in you based on what you said, and you are misusing it. That's also a lie.

"People have a tendency to lie so much, they don't even ask God to forgive them anymore because they now believe some lies are 'justified.' They would say things like, 'I didn't want to hurt her feelings, so I just lied and said I liked the dress.'

"Telling lies is more palpable, as it doesn't feel as bad as murder or worshiping false gods. I have searched the Bible, and I don't see where the Father has said that this sin is okay, but that sin isn't. He said that all have sinned and have come short of the glory of God.

The Pastor thought, "I've got to remember to preach a sermon on lies," realizing he hadn't before. Aloud, he said, "That's right, Son."

"Pastor, do you remember when you started telling lies?" the young man inquired.

"Oh, yes. When I was a child, we told little lies to keep from getting in trouble. I remember telling a story to my mother once. She told me she wasn't spanking me for what I had done; she said she was spanking me for the lie I had told. I didn't understand that at the time, but I did when I got older. I always wondered why lying was the first thing I thought to do when I was young."

The young man said, "I understand why our initial action turns to wrongdoing. The lie is a self-preservation mechanism. It's not the right thing to turn to, but it is in man's nature, as man was born into a sinful nature. This is why it's so easy for man to gravitate toward it.

"But we must learn to resist it. A lie won't always get you out of trouble; what it will do is separate you from the Father.

The more you lie, the more separation from God occurs because He said, 'A liar cannot tarry in my sight.' Telling lies puts a wedge between your relationship with God and yourself.

"I'm concerned, Pastor, that lies have become so prevalent that people don't deem them to be sins anymore. How do I help people bridge their relationships with God if I can't get them to honor Him with the truth?"

"So, this is your challenge, Son?" the pastor asked.

"Yes, Pastor," the young man said. "That's the challenge. People lie as they did as children. Many will say they are saved and filled with the Holy Spirit, and in their very next breaths, they will tell lies. They don't seem to understand that there is a separation going on here. I want to share with people that they need to trust in the truth, and God will help them overcome things if they just stop lying and move closer to Him.

"When I speak of this, Pastor, people laugh, telling me about the gray areas of lies. It is my challenge to eradicate this cavalier attitude people have regarding the sin of lying."

"Well, good luck, Son. I have been preaching for more than thirty years, and I have yet to make people turn away from lying."

"Oh, Pastor, but I believe that it doesn't start with the masses. I think it should start with the individual. And once the individual holds himself accountable, it will be like a chain reaction. People will then look at him and say, 'If he could do it, I can, too,' and another will say he can, as well. Pastor, I believe it all starts with the one and not the many."

"Well, that's a good concept, Son," the pastor agreed. "Maybe I can include that in one of my sermons—that it starts with one and not with many."

"Let's take you for instance, Pastor, because so many people hold you in such high regard."
"Yes, well..." The pastor began to puff up, smiling. "I've been faithful."

"Yes, Pastor, I agree. I have a question for you, and please don't take it the wrong way. I am just trying to teach myself how to put these things in perspective."

"No problem, Son. I'm here to help."
"Pastor, when was the last time you told a lie?"
The pastor cleared his throat abruptly. "Me?"
"Yes, Pastor. When was the last time you can remember that you told a lie?"

The pastor thought, "This boy is sharp." He had to be careful how he answered this question.

"Well, uh, I can't rightly say, Son. I guess it's like you said earlier: sometimes people will lie and don't even realize they're lying."

"I understand that, Pastor. But when was the last time you can envision yourself lying, be it by commission or omission, by your actions or by your inactions?"

The pastor began to think about his upcoming rendezvous with a certain young lady, and he thought about what the young man said about lying by actions.

"Well, Son, like you said, we've all sinned and come short of the glory of God. But the good thing about it is that we can pray and ask for His forgiveness, and He will forgive us seventy times seven in a day. That should cover any and all lies that may have cropped up."

"I agree, Pastor, but God is no fool. If you go out and steal something and ask God to forgive you, and then you go out and steal again and again, will you be forgiven? God looks at the heart to see if you're truly sorry and if you want to be forgiven. If you choose to continue in sin, He realizes that you're not really sorry for your actions. This is who you are becoming; this is your character. And all the prayers in the world will not save you.

The Storyteller Collection

"When a person lies and then asks God to forgive him or her, the slate is clean. But if the person continually goes out and lies, is he or she really asking for forgiveness? Or is this person just playing it safe with God, hoping that there is a safety net? That safety net is salvation from repentance. Did you forget the passage where God said, 'Now go, and sin no more'?

"We have to obey God and go back to one of the commandments: 'Thou shalt have no other god before me.' I believe, Pastor, that the magnitude of telling lies to save yourself puts lies akin to being your own god and your own savior, because lies are the first thing you call upon to rescue you. When you tell the lie and it appears it is taken for truth, the first thing you say is, 'Whew! I got out of that one.' You begin to feel that the lie kept you safe and sound, and you're literally treating the lie like your savior.

"Pastor, I believe we need to break this stranglehold that lies have on us, or we will all perish. We have to start with one another. We have to confess our sins, and God said that telling lies is a sin.

"The Father knew that we were born into sin, so it doesn't surprise Him when a little one says that he didn't break the window.

God covers the child's sin because he has no knowledge of the extent of the wrong he is doing. But once we reach ages at which there is full knowledge of the truth, then the sin of lies is on us and not on the Father.

"When you know that stealing is a sin, when you know murder is a sin, and when you know that using God's name in vain is a sin, it is now on your head to be responsible and repent, not justify it for the sake of safety.

"Of all the commandments, lying is the one most often broken. It has become part of people's natures. People don't feel convicted when they tell lies. And when they ask God's forgiveness of their sins, they don't include lies, because they know they are not done with the lying yet.

"Lies seem to be so prevalent that one can't seem to remember some of the lies one has told. But whether we lie to protect ourselves or lie to protect someone else, it is still a lie. We can paint lies to be pink, white, or shades of gray, but underneath the attempt to distort, the lie is still there.

"So, tell me, Pastor. How can I help people turn away from this particular sin? I believe that, once they eradicate this sin from their lives, all others will fall into place. When one stops lying, he or she will stop stealing. When one stops lying, one won't murder.

The Storyteller Collection

When one stops lying, one will hold God in high esteem. When one stops lying, one will respect his or her neighbors and hold them in high regard. When one stops lying, one will learn to respect himself or herself."

The pastor, once again trying to avoid this sticky situation, said, "Son, I know why you're confused a bit. The Ten Commandments are in the Old Testament. That was under the old law. In the New Testament, Jesus changed those old laws to just two, and things are different now, under the new regime."

But the young man would not relent, as he said, "Pastor, I beg to differ. It's true that, when the apostles asked which of all the commandments one are the ones we should adhere to most, Jesus said that there were two commandments that were far more important than all the rest: to love God with all your heart and your soul and your mind. Now, if you think about that commandment, you'll notice that it covers the first five commandments in the Old Testament. If you truly love God, you will not have any other god before Him; you will not worship false idols. You will not misuse His name, and you will remember His Sabbath and keep it holy.

"If you say you really love Him, you will honor your mother and father on earth like you will honor him in heaven. Do you see how that one commandment covers the first five commandments in the Old Testament? And the next commandment states that you should love your neighbor as yourself; this covers the last five. As we know, Jesus wasn't talking about your next-door neighbor; he was talking about your fellow man—your husband, your wife, your son, your daughter, your father, your mother, your friend, and even your enemy.

"For, if you love your neighbor—your fellow man—you will not kill him, nor engage in an adulterous relationship with his spouse. You will not lie or steal from him. And if you truly love and respect him, you won't covet what is not yours to have. Jesus made it clear that He wasn't here to change the laws but to give people a better understanding of the law and to save mankind.

"If man will adhere to these two commandments, they will adhere to *all* the commandments."

The pastor sat back and looked at this young man. He had been preaching for more than thirty years, yet this child had just taught him something. He had never known that all ten of the commandments were wrapped up in the two new commandments that Jesus gave. Why didn't he know that?

"Pastor, I feel that my calling is to make sure that others do not go to hell based on lies.

They must understand the true ramifications of their actions in telling lies. Lies are addictive, like drugs. It gives you a euphoric feeling when you feel you have escaped any type of prosecution for your actions. But just like drugs, it eats away at the heart of you, at your character, and it leaves nothing but a shell of a person without any credibility, trust, or worth in the eyes of others. A liar is labeled as a liar forever. In time, one's character can be restored, but one's credibility could be lost forever. Is lying to one's family or lying to one's congregation really worth it? People will take lying lightly, but a lie can send a person straight to hell."

All of a sudden, the pastor, without admitting guilt, felt convicted for his brand of lies. The pastor thought of his wife and how he had lied to her. He had told her he needed privacy to work on his sermon, but that was not true. That was the only instance for which he didn't have to account for his time, and he had wanted to see the young lady he had become fond of.

He had lied to the young woman, saying, "This is not a fling—this is real. I just need time to figure all this out." He had lied to his congregation; his heart was never in what he preached.

It was a show to see how much money he could squeeze out of his congregation.

He had become accustomed to thousand-dollar suits, million-dollar residences, and fabulous vacations. Someone had to pay for all that.

After having just heard the young man state that lying is intertwined with stealing, the pastor was more troubled. With beads of sweat having sprouted on his head, he rose from his chair and walked to the window. He was now taking no notice of the time, for once, as he said, "Lying is so cultural in our society. How does one stop lying?"

The young man said, "You can't; that's God's job. You pray and ask the Father to deliver you from evil and lying. And yes, lying is a form of evil, so you need to ask God to forgive you and break the bonds of lying. Let me assure you that God is faithful. He will do it. He will deliver you from lies."

Epilogue

Well, it had been exactly one month since the Pastor had set foot in the pulpit. He had some things to straighten out before he allowed himself back. That night, after he parted company with the young man, he knew he had to make some things right.

He was filled with trepidation as he drove over to the young woman's apartment. He felt like a child caught with his hand in the cookie jar, but he was determined to come clean.

As he left the young lady's apartment, he felt that he had been through the wringer. It wasn't easy to tell someone you had been lying to her and that you wanted to apologize. It didn't surprise him that she refused his apology and ordered him out. He deserved her anger and understood her pain.

He was a pastor. How could he bring her to Jesus with the lies he had told her? Now, he understood when the young man spoke of the loss of credibility.

He was going home and dreaded this most of all. His instinct was to just not say anything to his wife and to let sleeping dogs lie. But if he did this, the actions of his lies would remain a wedge between him and God, and he could live like that no longer.

It took two weeks before his wife would even speak to him again. She felt hurt and betrayed. She had been a good wife, and now, she was second-guessing herself. He had to reassure her that it was not her character that was lacking; it was his. He was asking her forgiveness daily and was willing to do anything to repair her trust in him.

After two weeks, she began to talk to him; she had questions. He was determined to be transparent and tell her the truth, even if it made him look worse.

He was nervous in the pulpit, and he had never been before in more than twenty-five years. Over the last month, he felt he had been beaten, mentally and emotionally. His children still weren't speaking to him. He realized that it would take time to gain back their trust and understanding. He was really coming to realize how lies damage every area of one's life.

The pastor looked out over the congregation; he was wondering what he could say to them. He was nervous and almost decided to change his mind. This was just too hard. He looked to the right in the front pews and realized that his wife was not there. His children weren't either. He had no safety net. But what did the young man say to him? "God doesn't give safety nets; He gives salvation."

So, with a deep breath, the pastor began to speak to the congregation. This day, he would have to lean on the compassion of Jesus. He had gotten himself into this with his lies, and he would have to get out of it with the truth.

His sermon, entitled "Telling Lies," was so difficult for him to preach because it was laced with his own lying, cheating, and stealing. He realized as he summed up his sermon that he now had no credibility, but he was determined to show them the way of insurrection is with the truth.

He told them that he understood if they no longer wanted him for their pastor, for what he had done was awful.

He wanted them to know and to understand that man will fail them, but God never will. He asked that they allow him to stay with the church in some minimal capacity, because he needed them more than ever before. He wanted them to know that he would be making full restitution for his stealing as well. He thanked the quiet crowd and quickly took his seat before he fell to the floor.

It was so quiet in the sanctuary that he thought someone had died. Finally, the assistant pastor stood and went to the podium. He then looked back at the pastor and began to clap. His clapping took on a life of its own, and it was in unison with the congregation.

"Pastor, we need you right here," said the assistant pastor, "for this church is not called 'Healed by Grace' for nothing. Today, we were taught about the perils of telling lies and how it attaches to even the highest in our congregation. Thank you for this lesson."

The Storyteller Collection

Salty tears rushed down the pastor's face. He didn't deserve what they were offering him, which was a second chance. This was true forgiveness.
As the congregation filed by the pastor and the assistant pastor, shaking their hands, they freely admitted their own struggles with telling lies, too. The pastor felt a sense of family and freedom to begin again.

Through the crowd, the pastor was looking for the young man, but he wasn't there. This was odd; he had not missed a Sunday in all the years the pastor had been there. He continued to look earnestly for him, to no avail, but he did see his parents, Meredith and Joe. He asked them if he could see them in his office for a moment.

Once the door had been closed behind them, they, too, told him how proud they were of him.
"I was looking for your son," the pastor explained. "I wanted to personally apologize to him for my actions."

Meredith and Joe looked at each other, perplexed. "Our...son?"

"Yes. I was frankly surprised; as this was the first time I've ever known him that he has missed a Sunday. Is he all right?"

Again, Meredith and Joe looked at each other, then Joe said, "Pastor, are you all right?

We don't have a son; you know that. We don't have any children."

It was the pastor who now looked confused. This must be some kind of a joke.
"Of course, you do. He has sat with you every service for the last twenty-one years. He was twelve when I first arrived here. I remember this, because he was the first to shake my hand."

"Pastor, we don't understand."
"Of course, you understand!" The pastor raised his voice. "He's here. He's always here. He works on the food committee, giving food to the poor. When we had the big fish fry dinner to feed the homeless, we ran out of fish, and he went and managed to get some from a local fish market. They not only gave him fish but a large supply of bread also."

"I don't remember us having a fish fry, Pastor."
"Well, how about the time when he called late one night, because a dozen of our teenage girls on a Night Lighting Expedition got lost? He had borrowed the church bus to pick them up. Some of them were so silly; their flashlight batteries went out."

The couple just shook their heads.
"Okay, I know the two of you were there with him the night we had our anniversary celebration and ran out of wine.

He was the one who went and told the hotel that we needed more. He was standing right next to you.

"He works for you, Joe, in your carpentry business! He just told me a month ago that he had decided to become an evangelist."
Meredith looked at her husband. "Joseph, he is frightening me."

"Mari, go on outside and wait for me." Joe calmed his wife. "I'll be there in a minute."
She nodded and left the pastor's office.
"Mari? You called her Mari?"

"Yes, it's a nickname; it's short for Meredith."
"But she called you Joseph."
"Pastor, that is my name, but some call me Joe."
"Joe, what do you do for a living?"

"I'm an electrician, Pastor; you know that. I have done work here in the church."

The Pastor's head was spinning. None of this made any sense to him. "You're telling me you don't have a thirty-three-year-old son?"

"No, Pastor, I assure you that my wife and I have no children. Pastor, you've had a lot of stress recently. Why don't you go home and get some rest? I'll lock up the church."

"Yes, maybe that's a good idea.

The Storyteller Collection

I don't know what has come over me. I was sure that I have known this young man since he was twelve years old."

As Joe headed out the door, he stopped for a minute and said, "You said you met a boy when he was twelve, and now he's thirty-three. This young man wanted to become an evangelist. He gave food to the poor and brought fish and bread to feed the homeless. He picked up twelve silly girls whose lights had gone out. He worked for his father as a carpenter and brought wine to a party..."

Slowly, the pastor said, "Yes." He began to rub his head as he walked over to the window. He had now put this all in perspective.

"Pastor, it sounds like to me that you were talking to Jesus."

End

The Storyteller Collection

Marie Browders'
The Storyteller©

The Friend

The Storyteller Collection

A friend loveth at all times.

Proverbs 17:17

The Friend

"Honey, you go on, and go to bed. I am too wound up to sleep. I will lock up," the chic, well-to-do woman said to her husband.

"I *am* bushed," her husband admitted, rubbing his hand tiredly through his hair like a comb. "I was so proud of you tonight. What an honor they bestowed upon you: the president of the clergymen's wives! You've worked hard to earn this acknowledgement, and there is no one prouder of you than I am."

"I was thrilled tonight, too. It feels like it has been a long time coming. I feel blessed and highly favored."

The clergymen gave his wife a loving kiss and headed for bed.

Since she was too excited to sleep, she decided to write a couple of letters of thanks before going to bed. In her kitchen, she poured herself a steaming brew of designer coffee as she checked the doors and set the alarm. She sauntered leisurely toward the back of her palatial home to her office.

She sought out her cushy slippers that she always kept in her office by the little sofa.

She replaced her elegant pumps with her slippers, shoving her feet in them with a quiet, swooshing sound. "Now, this is true comfort," she thought.

Sipping her steamed brew, she settled down from the excitement of the evening a bit. She was just the president of over two hundred clergy wives. This was big; this benefit tonight had been given in her honor. She had been on several boards through the years, but this was truly the most prestigious. She really had been blessed ever since she had turned her life over to Christ, and she was glad that she had.

Over the past eleven years or so since she had made that decision, she had not once missed her old life of drinking, partying, and drugs—not one bit. It seemed like a lifetime ago that she had walked away from it all back into what she had been taught as a child. She gave a slight shiver at the thought of some of the things she used to do and with whom she used to do it. But that was then, and this was now. Now, she was a pastor's wife and the assistant to the bishop's wife, who handpicked her and nominated her for this prestigious position as president. The bishop's wife was the first she wanted to thank, just after God. Her mind kept rolling back to those old days.

It always seemed to do this when she hit milestones in her life. She felt that it was just her yardstick, telling her how far she had come.

In nine years, she never shared her past with her husband. When she had asked God to forgive her of her sins, she didn't feel she needed to rehash it again. She had just wanted to put it all behind her and to look forward to her future at the time. Besides, she married a minister who was held in high esteem. What would he have thought of her if he knew of her other life? She shuddered to think how he would look at her if he had known some of the things she had been involved in back then.

From the beginning, she had known how badly her husband wanted children. What would he think of her three abortions or of the one daughter she had given birth to, whom she had given to an old friend without a second thought? She had damaged her body to the point that she could longer get pregnant again. At the time, that was all right with her, but now she wished she could undo all that and give her husband a child.

He wanted them be checked out to see why they weren't getting pregnant, but she couldn't let that happen; he might discover her past, so she told him they needed to pray and wait on the Lord. He finally agreed with her.

He truly thought that she was next door to a virgin when they married, since she was childless. If he had known about her life of wild parties and prostitution, she felt that he would not have looked at her twice.

She had prayed and prayed for forgiveness, until she felt she had received it and went on with her life—a life she cherished now with all her heart.

Shaking the past from her head, she pulled out a piece of lovely stationery to start her thank-you letters, when a small, nondescript note fell onto the floor. She picked it up and looked at it. It had no postage on it, just a singed mark on the corner. Her name was on it, but it was not her real name; it had her old nickname on it—the one she used back...then. It had been her old street name. There was no address on it; was this some kind of a joke? Apprehensively, she tore open the envelope to reveal what was inside.

She sat back, trying to catch her breath. It was from a friend—an old friend from back in the day. She said she had just arrived in town; she would be here for only one night, and she would like to stop by.

"Good lord," she thought; she had not even thought of her friend for almost twelve years.

Though she thought about her former life every now and then, she had put her friend and that whole life behind her the day she walked away after witnessing a murder. That seemed to turn her whole life upside down. It was the thing that had made her take stock of what she was doing out there. It had made her feel her own mortality. That was the day when, with just the clothes on her back, she had walked out of that life.

Now, someone from her past was back and wanted to see her. Why, for heaven's sake? Granted, they had been best friends back then. They had done everything—good and bad—together, but that was then; this was a new day. She was now the president of the clergymen's wives. She was nothing like she had been before. She hobnobbed with the elite now. She headed big fundraisers and charities for the local communities. If she met with her friend after all these years, she wouldn't know what to say to her.

No, meeting up with her was out of the question. She would send her a note apologizing but stating that she could not meet.

That was when it dawned on her that the note had no return address. And how had it made its way into her house and onto her desk? It hadn't been there when they left that evening. Had this former friend been in their home?

The Storyteller Collection

Was she *still* in her home?

She was so deep in thought over this that the knock on the French doors in her office startled her. The knock came again, harder this time. She didn't want her husband awakened, so she hurried to the door, turned off the alarm, and opened it.

It was her old friend. She bid her to come in. She couldn't quite see her friend's face, as it was covered by a dark shroud, but she remembered her voice like it was yesterday. She seemed tired and worn; the woman thought, "That's what that life will do to you." She wondered if her friend wanted money. That's it; she must've seen her on the cover of something and sought her out for money. Well, she and her husband were very comfortable, but she wasn't about to be blackmailed for the next twenty years.

"No," the friend said, as though she were reading her mind. "I did not come for money. It won't do me much good now."

"Well...I was just thinking...uh, have a seat." Now, she was perplexed, especially as her friend had just read her mind.

She declined. She chose to walk a bit around the office, looking at all the accolades her friend had acquired down through the years.

The Storyteller Collection

"You seem to have made a good life for yourself."
"Well, yes, I have been blessed. What about you? How've you been?"

"I don't think you really want to know."
"It's been years since we've seen each other. Are you still 'working' on Fifth Street in that city, where we used to live?"

"No. That has been over for quite a while. I live in a warmer climate now."

"I see." She really didn't. Her friend hadn't come for money, so why had she come?

The friend ran her hand across a well-crafted furniture piece. "Do you remember how we would dream of getting out of the life? How we made a pact that we would not leave each other behind?"
"I remember that we said a lot of things when we were high." She was being truthful.

"You're right. But we said this more often than not: we would always have each other's backs."
"Okay; I remember that we would say that. What does that have to do with today?"

"Do you remember the night of the...murder?"
How could she forget? They had been invited to an intimate party, just she and her friend and these two men in a swanky hotel room uptown. The drinks and drugs were flowing freely.

She and her friend had gone into the bathroom to hide the money they had been paid in their clothes when they heard a ruckus and shouting, and then they heard shooting.

Her friend, using her street smarts, had turned the light out in the bathroom and cracked the door wide. They hid behind it so that anyone looking would think no one was in there. They heard someone do a cursory look around the place, but, thankfully, the person did not go into the bathroom. She didn't know how long they stayed in there, but it seemed like an eternity.

When they were sure no one was there, she had eased out of the bathroom. When she saw the bodies on the floor, a scream welled up in her throat, but her friend clamped her mouth shut. Her friend quickly went about, wiping their fingerprints off anything they had touched in the room. She didn't want anyone to know they had been in there.

Her friend then cracked the door to make sure no one was in the hall, and they eased out into the hallway and closed the door. She tried to get her head wrapped around what had happened but, she couldn't. Her friend wasn't as inebriated as she was, and she got both of them out of there in a hurry.

On the drive home, she began to sober up and realized what had happened, even though she couldn't remember the particulars. The full realization of what her life was turning into hit her like a sledgehammer.

"Are you all right?" her friend asked, truly concerned for her welfare.

"Yes. I'm all right," she said quietly.
Her friend and the baby had the bedroom in their one-bedroom apartment. As she laid on the sofa, she couldn't sleep. She could have been killed, too. What if that person had decided to search the hotel room to give it more than a cursory glance? Sweaty and not able to sleep, the woman threw the covers back, got out of bed and began to pace.

Years ago, she had thought her parents too old-fashioned for her. She had wanted excitement and fun, and, over the four years she had been out there, she had had that. But what had just occurred gave her a rude awakening, and she began to feel that she no longer wanted this life. She had been brought up in the church. She had known Jesus all of her life. She wanted Him back again...she wanted to go home.

She eased down on her knees (she had not been on them since she had left home), and then, she began to pray. She prayed slowly at first, hesitantly and embarrassed.

She had done so much wrong that she felt He would never forgive her. She had had two abortions, and she would have had one with this child, except that she had been too far along this time to do anything about it. She had so much to ask Jesus' forgiveness for; she could hardly hold her head up. She stayed on her knees until dawn.

When she finally got up, she felt different; she felt kind of new and free. Old desires began to sink in, and she wanted to see her parents. She had avoided that since she had left home, but she would call from time to time.

She thought for a moment to wake her friend and tell her that she had decided to go back home, but why? Her friend's life was here. According to her, she had always been here.

She knew that, even if she decided to go with her, she couldn't support her or the baby. And what would her parents say to all of this? No—she didn't want anyone to know of her life here on the streets. Her decision was made as she quietly dressed. She scribbled a little note saying she that had decided to go home and left. After all these years, she never looked back, and there were times when she would think it all a dream.

"Of course, I remember. How could I forget?" she rasped. "That was why I left."

"I figured as much," her friend conceded. "It got to me, too. When I woke, I wanted to ask you about getting out of the life, but you were already gone."

"So, did you?" The woman hesitated, inwardly thinking that it was none of her business.
"Did I what?" her friend asked.

"Did you leave the life?" She couldn't help herself.

"Yes. The same day you did," she answered. "The baby and I first went to a shelter and then a halfway house for my drug addiction, where they allowed me to keep her with me. After a year, I managed to get a job and an apartment in another city. We have been there this whole time and...we've been happy."

"I'm glad." She didn't believe her, as she looked withdrawn, old, and worn-out. Her clothes appeared dirty and torn. "No," the woman thought, "something else is up."

"So, be honest. Why did you come?" The woman felt that there was no use in beating around the bush.

"I want two things. I want you to tell me about this Jesus." She held her head down. "I just want to know what He is all about."

The Storyteller Collection

"You can find that out at any local church." She wanted her to go.

"No. I never will; that is why I want to know about Him. I don't have much time. This is your line of business, isn't it? Tell me what you would tell some sinner in your church."

She just wouldn't relent, so the woman said, "Almost from the beginning of time, people waited for Him for to come. He was our deliverer, the Promised One, who was sent down to earth to save us from our sins and keep us from going to hell. When He came, people thought He would show up as a king, but He was born in a manger from humble beginnings. He wanted people to know that He was everyone's Savior and that He was not just for the elite.

"When He was older, He began to preach and teach everywhere. He also healed people mentally, physically, and spiritually."

"So that's all He did? Just preach like every other preacher? Like those on television?"

"No, He was different. He is the only one who can save you from hell. When you pray to Him and ask Him for forgiveness, He will save you from all your sins. That night, after what...we saw, I prayed and asked Him to forgive my sins, and He did."

"So that is the difference between Him and all those storefront preachers? This forgiveness thing?"

"The difference is this: if you pray and ask Him to forgive you your sins, He is faithful, and He will." She clarified, "If it is so important for you to know and to understand Him, why don't we pray together now?"

"No, no!" she said. "It's too late for me now."
"What do you mean, it's too late?" The woman was confused. "As long as you're alive, it's never too late."

"That's what I mean." She turned and walked to the other side of the room slowly. "I...uh...died tonight."

"You...what?!" This wasn't true; the woman could see her friend right before her eyes.

"It's true. I worked in a market, and I was on the night shift. When my shift was over, I wanted to hurry home, pick up our daughter from the sitter, and get her out of the night air. I was thinking about an outfit I had to make her for a play at school and walked behind a moving vehicle that didn't see me. My body is in the emergency room now."

"Good lord!" the woman gasped. "Dead?"

"It all happened so fast that I didn't realize it myself."

"Let's pray together, now, before it's too late! Please, let me do something for you."

"It's already too late for me, but it's not for our little girl. She is only ten years old. She's got to have a chance to stay out of hell. You didn't help me when you could, but I'm begging you and your Jesus to help her."

The woman began to look at her friend with new eyes. Even now, when everything was against her, she was trying to remain a friend. The woman saw no bitterness in her, just a sorrow, as she wished that she had known more about Jesus than she did. The woman knew that her friend's knowledge back then had been very dim, yet she had never spoken a word of what she knew of Jesus and salvation. Now it was too late; her friend was dead. "Oh, Lord," she silently cried out, "why didn't I think of helping her back then, when she had a chance? Why didn't I tell your story—that only through your glory would she be safe, for she would have been saved?"

Her friend had taken on her responsibility and never shirked it. She had taken care of her child when she could not take care of herself.

The Storyteller Collection

The woman knew her friend's life story; at the time, she just hadn't cared. She knew that her friend had grown up in foster homes. When she was twelve and she could no longer stand the groping hands of her foster fathers, so she had started to make her life on the streets. Who was there to teach her of the everlasting love of Jesus? Who would have told her of the scripture that stated that God so loved this world of ours that He gave His only begotten Son, and whoever believes in Him would never perish but have everlasting life? (*This scripture was found in John 3:16.*)

Pain and sorrow cut through her like a knife as her friend said, "She's almost the same age I was when I hit the streets. I don't want that to happen to her. She's a good little girl; one of our neighbors takes her to church with her and taught her nightly prayers, too. But I want you to teach her how to be saved. I don't want her to succumb to my fate."

The woman wanted to hug her friend, but when she tried, her friend backed away. "I don't want you to have the stench of death on you. We have a pact now, right?"

The woman nodded her head. "I am so sorry for the wrong I've done you. And I want to thank you for taking care of my...our...little girl."

"Another thing. Don't tell her I died. I don't want her to be sad.

"Tell her that I had to go away and she is to be the good little girl I know she can be. The address where she can be found is in the note." With that, the friend backed away into the shadows.

The woman fell to her knees, crying wretched tears. She thought, "Why her, Lord? Why not me? Even in death, she was kind to me." The woman sobbed herself to sleep right on the floor, at the feet of Jesus...

"Honey!" Her husband shook her. "You feel asleep on the floor. Are you all right?"

She was groggy and shaken. Had it all been a dream or maybe even a nightmare? Had she really dreamed all of this? Her husband helped her unsteadily to her feet. Light streamed brightly through her office windows. It was another day.

"I'm okay, honey, just overly exhausted from the events of last night," she said, too brightly. "Let me go and wash my face. Will you pour me a cup of coffee?"

Her husband left from the room, and she went into the hall bathroom and threw cold water on her face. The water seemed to do the trick. As she walked past her office toward the kitchen, the brown, non desscript letter caught her eye once more.

She retrieved it from her desk and realized that last night had been real!

This was her letter, with no postage on it. Shakily, she opened it wide, and an address fell out of it, along with a picture of the most beautiful and precocious little girl. She had pigtails with blue ribbons falling on either side of her cheeks. She had deep dimples, like the woman's, and beautiful brown eyes.

She was well taken care of; she could see that. But who was to care for her now? Could she? She just didn't know. If she spoke of the child, she would have to speak of her past as well. Was she ready to jeopardize everything for which she had worked, as well as a loving husband, who doted on her, and parents, who loved her dearly?

She couldn't bear to have everyone think less of her, as she did herself. She walked into the kitchen, clutching the letter tightly, and sat across from her husband. "Dear?" was her preamble. "I have something to tell you..."

He glanced up from his morning paper for a moment and then back up again swiftly, as he saw his wife of nine years crying before him. "What's the matter? Tell me."

"We have to go quickly," she gushed out, "My best friend died last night, and we have to go and get my daughter."

Epilogue

It had been two years since her friend had died and since they went and picked up her daughter. She was surprised at the fact the child knew she was her mother. Her friend had always kept the woman alive in her daughter's heart and mind.

The child was inquisitive, as she should have been, questioning her about her "aunt." The woman, however, made a promise to her friend that she would never tell her daughter that her friend had died not knowing Jesus and had gone to hell.

That was the hardest of it all for her. Her friend had been the sweetest and most giving person, and she had never realized it. Her heart had always been in the right place, and, if situations were turned around, she knew in her heart that her friend would have taken her with them.

She had learned an awful lesson that night two years ago; self-preservation is fine, but when others throw you a lifeline, you need to not forget it. Once you reach safety, you should throw it back to help the one who saved you.

We are truly all our brothers' and sisters' keepers. People are more precious than how one looks in the eyes of others. And that day, her husband had surprised her. He didn't question her, as he knew she would share when the time was right.

The Storyteller Collection

He held back his surprised at learning of a child of whom he had never known.

He drove her directly to a particular address. He could tell that she was surprised that the little girl knew her on sight, as her friend had given her a picture. She had said, "I know who you are; my aunt told me—you're my mother."

She had looked up at her husband with fresh tears in her eyes, and he just smiled down at her, saying, "Let's go home with our daughter."

The woman was cleaning out her daughter's closet one day when she noticed a small box at the top. She thought, "Oh, this is one of the things she brought with her two years ago." She opened it and saw little trinkets and keepsakes in it, and there was also a picture of her friend in there.

"Are these from your aunt?" she asked her when her daughter walked in the room.

"Some are," she said offhandedly, "but the picture of my aunt is from Jesus."

She eyed her daughter and then looked at the picture of her friend again. She looked beautiful and happy. It must have been an earlier picture of her. "Honey, are you sure Jesus gave this picture to you?"

"Yes, Mom." She was sure. "He came the same night my aunt went away. Jesus wanted me to have something to remember her by. He gave me her picture. He took it. Isn't she beautiful?"

The woman now knew she would have to address this absence of her friend. It was long overdue. "About your aunt…when she had to go away…"
"I know all about that. Jesus told me."
"Jesus? What did He tell you?"

"The night before you came for me, He came by and sat on my bed. He told me not to be afraid because He loved my aunt and wanted her to go and live with Him. He told me not to worry, because my mother was back, and she was coming to get me in the morning."

"He told you that?" Tears began to cloud up her eyes.

"Yes. He said He had heard all the prayers I had prayed since I was little for my aunt, and He wanted me to know that He heard me and that my aunt was going to be all right with Him. I knew my aunt didn't know how to pray, so I prayed for her."

End

The Storyteller Collection

The Letter

My friend, I stand in judgment now...
and feel that you're to blame somehow.
While on this earth, I walked with you day by day.
And never once did you point the way.

You knew the Lord in truth and glory,
but never did you tell the story.
My knowledge then was very dim,
you could have led me safe to Him.

Though we lived together here on earth,
you never told me of your second birth.
And now I stand this day condemned...
because you failed to mention Him.

I taught you many things, that's true;
I called you friend and trusted you.
But I've learned...now that it's too late...
you could have kept me from this fate.

We walked by day and talked by night,
and yet you showed me not the light.
And let me live, love, and die,
and all the while you knew I'd never live on high.

Yes, I called you friend in life,
and trusted you in joy and strife...
And yet in coming to this end...
I see you really weren't my friend.
—D. J. Higgins

The Storyteller Collection

Dear Friend

You were right! I was not your friend.
A friend would've loved you to the end.
I should've told you of Jesus' story,
and showed you the way into His glory.

I should have told you of the Virgin Birth,
that came to save us here on Earth.
But a word of that, I never uttered,
and now you're where you shouldn't ought to.

But Lord, please forgive me for this sin,
and allow me to show others the way in.
Never again will I shirk my mission,
to show others away from their transgressions.

I know this will not help, my friend,
for once dead, judgment begins.
But let me share my sad, sad story,
to help people realize only through Your glory,
will they be safe, for they'll be saved,
and never again will they fear the grave.

For God so loved the world, this is true,
that Jesus came down and died for you.

So remember this story of me and my friend,
and let not what happened here happen again;
Because now you've been told…
now you know better;
I pray you'll not receive—a similar letter.
Signed: the forgiven friend.
© 2000 Marie Browders

The Storyteller Collection

The Storyteller Collection

Words

The Couple

"I am sick of you constantly demeaning my character!" the wife rasped. "This has got to stop!"
"You're sick of the way I demean you? Didn't you just say to me that I was weak and useless as man?" the husband countered. "How do you think that makes me feel?"

"Well, it appears that the shoe fits!" the wife retorted, clearly upset.

"If you think I'm useless, what about you?" the husband countered. "Being married to you has not been a walk in the park, frankly. I am trying to figure out why I'm still in it!"

"Because you're not man enough to do what you always threaten to do: leave."
"Oh, I'm man enough," he shot back, "I just stayed because I felt sorry for you. After I leave, you'll have nothing and no one.

You can't even get pregnant!"
He had really hit her where it hurt now. They had been married for thirteen years, and they had tried everything to start a family.

They had finally gone to get tested and found that her fallopian tubes had never fully developed, and she would never give birth. The doctor had told him he was perfectly fine and could produce offspring. This had been six years ago, and she had felt every day since then that he blamed her for his inability to become a father. He knew where to aim the arrow and shoot with precision.

"I knew you blamed me for you not being a father," she spat at him. "Don't worry about me; I will not be single long. Go on out there, and populate America. Someone would let you be the father of her child: a man who can't keep regular money coming in to help support a family. You will definitely get the Father of the Year award in no time!"

Oh, he wanted to push her face in. That was a low blow.

She had been able to secure a college degree, while he worked to support them both, and now, career opportunities were better for her than for him. Their plan was that he would send her to school first, and then, while she worked, he would then go to back to college.

But after she obtained her degree, everything changed. She worked with high-powered people, and she began to think him beneath her.

He just continued to work, but his job opportunities were not as prevalent as hers. She knew that this bothered him, along with the fact that she broke their pact in this area. He refused to beg her to support him while he went to college full-time.

"You know, this conversation, like this marriage, is over!" he retorted. "I'm glad that, after tonight, I never have to see your dried-up face again!"

She turned away from him; he had to have the last blow. He had to intimate the truth that she was ten years older than he.

The husband walked around the bed toward the door. He was going to go and sleep in the den, but stubbornness prevailed, and he turned, went to his side of the bed, threw back the covers, sat down, and thrust his legs under the covers, turning away from her.

She felt that she could not sleep in the same bed as her husband, but he would not make her leave her bedroom, either, so she got into bed, turning away from him as well.

The couple could not agree on many things these days, but they did agree on one thing after that night: divorce!

The wife felt that the husband really hurt her deeply, and there was no way to heal what he put her through that night.

The husband felt that he had had it. He had paid for her education. When the market tanked and he had found himself out of a job, she had looked down on him like he was nothing. He wanted a wife, not a cold-hearted executive. He would call an attorney first thing in the morning.

As he tried to drift off to sleep, he was dividing all the assets they had accumulated over thirteen years of marriage. "What a waste," he thought, as sleep finally caught up with him, and he was gone on the journey of his life…and hers, too.

The Wife

As the wife slumbered, her dream took her to a calming place: a small, rock-filled mountain, just outside of a town that looked like…Bethlehem?

"This is something I have never dreamed of before," she thought, as she walked toward the town. Upon entering into this gate-free town, she noticed that there were a lot of people in the town.

Quite a few were circulating; many were sleeping, it appeared, wherever they could. They were sleeping on the sides of buildings, leaning against walls, and in alleyways.

What were they all here for? But Bethlehem, she then remembered, had its first official census back then. She remembered the story of Joseph having to register in the place of his father's birth for the census. She remembered that, though quite pregnant, Mary had decided to accompany him there. Yes, these people all looked like travelers, so this must have been that instance.

Well, if her dream had taken her to Bethlehem, she wondered if she would get a glimpse of the baby Jesus, lying in a manger, clothed in swaddling rags. She looked around for the stables, but she saw nothing.

She continued down the center of the town, looking for where they kept the livestock. Finally, at the end of the long main road, she noticed that fewer and fewer people were about; finally, even farther down, she saw no one. She did, however, smell the aroma of horse manure and felt she was getting close.

She turned down a small, nondescript road and eyed a big, cavernous place, where the livestock were. This stable was built in the side of a small mountain, and there, the livestock was tied up.

As she adjusted her eyes to the darkness, the wife saw a hint of light coming off a ledge over the far side of the stable; she then saw Mary sitting next to a manger that was filled with hay and rags, holding the baby Jesus ever so gently.

In this setting, the wife found that the humiliating argument and divorce resolution seemed to fade away, as she beheld such a sight. Mary was sitting on a mound of hay, cradling her child protectively in her arms. Looking at this scene, she could tell that Mary was going to make a wonderful mother.

Mary glanced up at the wife and smiled as she motioned her over. The wife did as she was requested, for just being in the presence of the Lord, at any age, had a profound effect on her life.

"Come closer," Mary urged the wife, smiling a simply lovely smile. The wife noticed that, against all accounts, Mary was not a pretty girl, as far as features were concerned. But the way she smiled and intermittently glanced down to her bundle of joy brought out an inner beauty that could not be denied.

"I—I don't want to disturb the baby Jesus," the wife whispered softly. "I have no children of my own, so this is a sight to behold."

"That's all right." Mary smiled at her. "In time, you will be a mother, and then you will know what a child does to your whole outlook on life."

"Thank you for those encouraging words, but I will never have a child," the wife said with a heavy heart. "Besides, it was tonight that my husband and I decided to divorce."

"I know." Mary sighed. "I heard the words the two of you said to each other, and it saddened me. You see, Jesus heard them as well. He was not pleased with how you and your husband utilized His gift to you of the power of words by setting them against each other."

"Did you hear the things he said to me?" the wife asked. "I have taken his angry words for the last time."

"I agree; this should be the last time that the power of words is used in this way." Baby Jesus began to fidget, and Mary gathered her precious child to her left breast, where he began to suckle contently. "Words are so powerful that our Lord took them away from Zachariah, my cousin's husband, when he did not believe in the fact that Elizabeth would bear a son. Words are deemed one of the most powerful gifts with which our Lord and Savior blessed us. However, our words cannot only destroy one's spirit but they also can inflict real wounds."

"I believe that, Mary," acknowledged the wife.

"My husband hurt me deeper than he ever had this night, and I cannot be married to him any longer."

"In the Holy Word, in Proverbs 18:21, it is said that 'the tongue has the power of life and death,' but I have not been called to preach to you. I am here to tell Joseph and my story to you."

"I forgot about Joseph," the wife said. "Where is he now?"

"He will return shortly," Mary assured the wife. "Our lovely child here has sent him on a small journey to speak to your husband."

"My husband?"

"Yes, your husband." Mary smiled and repositioned the child to her other breast. "So, let me share my story with you about my journey with my husband.

"I was not a direct descendent of King David, but Joseph is. I was just a simple girl of no consequence, I felt. I was born and raised in Nazareth. Joseph, a skilled carpenter, came to our village and set up shop a year earlier. He was tall and handsome, and many women would have been proud to be his wife. I was thrilled to no end when he asked my parents for my hand in marriage, as was the custom of the time."

The Storyteller Collection

Mary had now gotten baby Jesus back to sleep, and she lay him gently back in the manger and covered him up with swaddling rags. "We were planning to have our wedding, as was the custom after our courtship. We had not been courting long when a vision came to me that I was the virgin who was chosen to be the mother of the Messiah.

"I had so many questions: would He be deemed illegitimate? Would Joseph still want me as his wife? But the Lord asked me if I trusted Him, and I was quick to say, 'Yes, Lord. I trust you.' At that moment, I knew all I had to do was trust in Him, and everything would be all right.

"I had a dream that my cousin was with child, and I needed to visit her. My parents and Joseph did not want me to go, but I felt I must, so I went. It was exciting for me, for I did not have to tell her that I was with child. She knew it!

"I stayed with her for three months and finally went home, exhilarant. I was so full of joy and grace that I truly forgot that my appearance had changed, and I was indeed filled with child. People in my village looked, disgusted, at me, but the Lord told me to just trust Him, and I did.

"I could, however, see the disappointment in Joseph's eyes when he saw me.

He wanted to know whom I had been with, and I assured him that I had been with no one. I could see that he did not believe me, and he turned and left. My parents were upset and scared as well, for they knew that Joseph had a right to have me stoned for my condition. For some reason, I had no fear of that.

"He came over the next day and asked my parents if he could speak to me in private. They gave permission warily. Once outside our small house, he gathered both of my hands and said that he had a dream and was told not to fear to take me as his wife. I looked in his eyes, and I could see that something had come over him. He said that we were to be married immediately, and we were.

"Not one time did he ever speak despairingly regarding my condition. He treated me as though I were a porcelain doll. He began to build a wonderful house in Nazareth—one with many rooms, for many children. Now, I know that he was still hearing wagging tongues as he went to work each day, but he chose to ignore them, and he never brought these comments back to me.

"One day, when I was in my later months of pregnancy, there was an order posted that they were starting a census and that every man must register.

He was going to have to make the journey back to Bethlehem, his hometown, alone and leave me with my parents.

"I petitioned to go along with him, and he finally relented. It was a long journey, and we had but one mule. He had me perched on it, and he walked over hills and valleys, being mindful to let me rest periodically. He would take some of our water that we had brought and would rub my face with it. On our journey, we talked and laughed. When he looked so exhausted, I would speak up and encourage him, letting him know how much I appreciated him for taking care of us. He would tell me that I was his wife and that it was his honor to care for me.

"With our encouraging words, we kept building each other up, until we completed our journey. We arrived in Bethlehem late in the evening. My back was aching tremendously, as I feared the birth was near and told Joseph so. But one thing we did notice was that the town was filled to capacity with people coming here for the same reason.

"We stopped at an inn; however, there was no room for us. Joseph went up and down the street, trying to locate a place for me to lie down, to no avail.

He then spoke in earnest to some people, 'Is there any place for us? My wife's time is upon us.'

"A compassionate person suggested the stable. A stable? Joseph wanted to refuse, but I tapped his shoulder, letting him know that we didn't have a choice. He then nodded his thanks and hurried to the end of town to the stable. It was so dark that he purchased a lantern from one of the merchants. He had me wait at the entrance while he found the best place in here, which was on this ledge. He pulled up several mounds of hay for me to lie on. He pulled a short trowel up on the ledge for the baby, feeling a bit down, wishing that he could do better for his family, but I just told him it was lovely.

"He carried me up on the wide ledge and lay me down on the straw. Pains were coming quicker, as he scoured wherever he could for some water and rags. He had to assist in this birth, but he was right there, encouraging me and consoling me until our child arrived.

"Once baby Jesus was here, he whispered to me, 'You are a wonderful woman, and you will make a wonderful mother.'

"What I wanted to share with you was that we went through some challenging times. He had every right to denounce me and have me stoned.

But he never said a disparaging word to me, nor I to him. We treated each other with love, kindness, and respect. Each encouraging word between us allowed us to trust each other more. I thank God for my husband. At this point, we have more challenges ahead of us, but I know that, together and with God's grace, we will conquer it all."

The wife had begun to tear up as she heard Mary and Joseph's story. She had heard it many times growing up, but it was different to hear Mary's voice rise and fall with each of their challenges. They never once fought against each other but had encouraged each other again and again and again. She felt that the first thing a marriage should have is trust.

It was important to trust each other and not to use intimate knowledge of each other as swords against them. She had been a fool. Instead of keeping to their plans once she was educated; she had looked down on her husband and didn't want to help him become educated, as he had done her. She so wanted to ask him for forgiveness for her part in their marriage's disintegration.

Even if they divorced, she wanted him to know that she was willing to make good on her promise regarding to his education.

"Well, I have told you my story," Mary said. "Joseph should be returning shortly. I pray that you've found some measure of wisdom that you can take back to your time. Grace be with you." Mary bowed and returned to caring for her child.

The Husband

The husband slept fitfully. He tossed and turned, until he felt the wings of slumber take him on a flight. He was glad to be dreaming; he felt his body loosening up and resting. His dream soared him in space and, more accurately, in time.

He found himself in a clearing overlooking a town—Bethlehem? He wiped his eyes and looked again in disbelief. Yes, it was Bethlehem. He thought, "This is a dream for the books!"

He sat down on a large stone and stared down at the town, thinking, "What am I to do here? Should I journey into the town and look around?" As he pondered his next step, he saw a figure of a tall man adorned in nondescript robes of gray and dusty brown. His head was covered with a turban, which was pulled down to the top of his beard. The husband noticed that it was extremely early in the morning and that the weather was cool.

"Greetings, in the name of our Lord, Jesus Christ," Joseph said, bowing a bit. "I am Joseph.

The Storyteller Collection

"Brother, may I sit with you a bit?" The husband nodded, wondering if this is the Joseph of "Joseph and Mary."

"Yes, to your question." Joseph could hear his nonverbal question. "Mary of Nazareth is my wife, and today is the birth of our son, Jesus. I have been sent on an errand to share with you some of the trials and tribulations of our marriage and how we overcame them."

"That's easy for you to say," grumbled the husband. "You married the perfect woman and had Jesus as your son. You should have heard the argument my wife and I had last night; it was brutal. We have decided to call it quits, and I am glad, because I cannot take this anymore."

"I was made aware of the words you spoke into existence earlier. They were unfortunate. You know the Lord said that though it is a gift, our words have the power to destroy or the power to build up." Joseph was referencing Proverbs 12:6. "Uh, I think I heard that somewhere," the husband lamented, "but she gave as good as she got!"

"You, my brother, will be held to a higher authority than she, because you are the head of your household," Joseph reminded him. "But I am not here to instruct you on how you rule your home; I am here to tell the story of Mary and me."

The Storyteller Collection

"You stated that we had a perfect marriage and a perfect son," Joseph said. "Please let me share some of our challenges with you."

"I am a direct descendant of King David. I was born here in Bethlehem, as was my father before me. I grew up here and learned the skills of a carpenter. With many skilled laborers here, I thought I would go to a small town, where business would be brisk, so I journeyed to Nazareth.

"It was a nice little town, and it was easy to start my business there. After being there for about a year, I took notice of this young woman with one of the sweetest smiles as I had ever seen. I said nothing initially; I just watched her, as she would pass my shop with other girls her age. I would notice her at times in meditation in the meadows as well as at times when she was praying. After a time, I had decided that I would like to marry her. As is our custom, I could not approach her until I had her parents' permission. So I sought her parents out and presented my prospects as a husband to them with my desire to start courting their daughter, Mary.

"Her father gave me permission and called Mary in. She was told of my desire to court her the allotted time and then marry her. She smiled brightly, stating that she was willing.

My heart almost leaped out of my chest, knowing she was as interested in me as I was her.

"Needless to say, our courtship began. I wanted to surprise her with a well-built home of our own. I wanted to have it completed by the time we were married.

"One day, I was called over to her parents' home, as she wanted permission to visit her cousin Elizabeth. I thought this odd, as we had only begun our courtship. How could we court when she was so far away? Since she was betrothed to me, I had a say in whether she was to be allowed to go or not. I had been busy with the business and with building the house, so I had little time for courting her, anyway. I gave my permission that she could see her cousin.

"It was odd; she was gone for three months. I was wondering when she would return. The home was almost completed; our nuptials were soon to be, yet there was no sight of my betrothed.

"After I thought this, the very next day, a neighbor came up to me, stating that Mary had returned. I smiled with gladness, but he seemed to have sadness in his eyes regarding the news. I did not put much stock in that; my Mary was back, and I had missed her so.

"She came to greet me before she greeted her parents. I went up to her, smiling. I was helping her off the mule when it became clear to me—she was with child!

"You said to me that she was 'perfect.'" Joseph said, "How would you like your virgin bride to come back from a long trip, visibly pregnant, when you knew the child was not yours?"

"I forgot about that part of your story, man," the husband said. "I'd rather have my wife barren than to come to me with a child not my own. Hey, didn't they stone women in your day who were in that predicament?"

"That is our custom, yes," Joseph acknowledged, "but in that instance, though I thought she had done me wrong, I loved her, and I wanted no harm to come to her. I had just made up my mind to put her away quietly, so that no harm would come to her.

"At that point, I was hurt and heartbroken, even though she assured me that she had done nothing wrong. I needed to be away from her at that time. I needed what you call in your time 'space.' That night, it was hard for me to sleep, with so many emotions twirling in my head. I wanted to find who had attacked her and make him pay.

"But an angel came to me in a dream and told me not to be afraid to take Mary as my wife. The angel told me that she was carrying the Messiah, who would take away the sins of the world. That next morning when I awoke, I felt joyful and happy. I believed what the angel had said to me. I hurried over to her parents' home and asked to speak to her in private. When we were alone, I told her of my dream and that I believed everything she had said. I told her that I still loved her and wanted to marry her now even more.

"She was so happy that she began to cry. Since the pregnancy was evident, I sought out clergy so that we could be married immediately. I wanted to minimize the wagging tongues. Marriage changes things. I was no longer making decisions just for myself; I had a family to care for.

"I wanted to finish the house for us, but that never came to fruition, as a notice came of the first census. Since I was not born there, I had to go to the place of my father's birth to register.

"I told Mary that she should stay with her parents until I returned, because she was so close to her time. She pleaded to accompany me on the journey, and I have to tell you, I did not want to be away when our child was born, so I relented.

"Two days into the journey, I thought I had made a big mistake by taking a woman in an advanced stage of pregnancy with me. She was exhausted. I made many stops along the way so that she could rest. I think that she could see the worry on my face regarding the journey, but she would just keep encouraging me along, saying how proud she was to have me as her husband and how much she loved the home I was building for us. Whenever I felt weak and unsure, there she was, lifting me up with her words. I must admit, I don't think I could have made it without her faith and trust in me.

"So, brother, we arrived here last night, and our child, Jesus, was born in these early hours.

"This was not a perfect situation or the beginning of a perfect marriage. But Mary and I continue to trust in the Lord and continue to speak words of kindness and encouragement to each other. My Mary deserves all I can do for her, and, by the grace of God, I plan on being a good husband to her for the rest of my life.

"I'm afraid you will have to forgive me, but I must get back to my family." Joseph stood and bowed slightly. "They are in need of me."

The man replayed Joseph's words in his head, as he saw him head back down in all haste to the town where his wife and child were. Joseph was right; he had gone through a bevy of emotions during his challenges with his wife, but not once had either of them attacked the other. Even through his worst time, when he found Mary pregnant, he did not demean her character.

The husband felt like he had just met a true man who was the head of his household. He thought of his own wife. He thought of the things he had said to her; they were inexcusable. He was blaming his wife for his own shortcomings. He was the head of their household. He didn't have to blame her for the lack of him beginning his education; he could go to school part-time while working. He could attend a trade school instead of college, which was shorter. He had always been interested in heating and air conditioning. Since he was the head of the family, he could make alternative decisions for the family.

The husband stood, with more resolve in him than ever before. He wanted to talk to his wife. He wanted to apologize to her for not taking his place as head of the household and let her know his plans for this family.

Once again, his dream took flight, returning him from whence he came.

The Couple

Where words can alter one's life, words can bathe one in second chances. The couple awoke and noticed that they were no longer apart but were facing each other.

The wife looked into her husband's eyes and saw the same love he had for her when she had found out that she was barren. She remembered that he had said, "Well, *we* can't have children, and that's that." He had never said *she* couldn't; he had said *they* couldn't. He had let her know then that their marriage together was more important. She loved him.

As he adjusted his eyes to the morning sun, looking at her, he was reminded that she had never once demeaned his character when he couldn't find work. She had just been there, supporting both of them.

How did they get to last night, when they wanted to draw emotional blood from each other? How had such cruel words spewed from their mouths? "Good morning," the husband greeted his wife. "Good morning to you, too." She smiled.

"I would like to apologize—" they both said in unison and then smiled.

"Okay, you go first." The wife snuggled a little closer to her husband.

"Okay, I would like to apologize for my behavior," he said. "As head of this household, it was up to me to set the tone of our relationship, and I did not.

The Storyteller Collection

I know words that are spoken cannot be taken back, but I would like to add an addendum to them: I love you. I have loved you for thirteen years, and I plan on loving you for the rest of my life. I am proud of your intelligence, and I will never put you down again. It was my responsibility to get you through college, and it is my responsibility to get myself through as well, and I will do it.

"I have decided to go to trade school at night and work during the day. I know I can do this. As of this day, you can trust me to lead this family and not push this family. You can trust me to care for you and protect you, for I will be doing it by the Lord's direction and not by my own personal agenda. So do you think you can possibly forgive me?"

The wife hugged her husband and said, "Only if you could forgive me. I now see that I was trying to usurp your position for myself, as I felt that money made you subservient to me, which was wrong. I am putting my trust in you to direct this family, as is your right."

Epilogue

Neither this man nor his wife had any right to ask the other to submit when they were arbitrarily expressing their own opinions, and their own selfish wills benefit only one side.

They needed to have a clear direction from God regarding what would be best for all concerned. Their obligation was to follow God's path and not their own.

Once they started to consult the Lord in every decision, spending time in prayer to seek His wisdom, searching the Word for His principles to guide them, and waiting for the assurance of His peace, they were then steering their marriage in the right direction.

By acquiescing to God's will, regardless of their own personal preferences, they knew that He would protect them from making grievous mistakes that brought unhappiness to a family.

Under these circumstances, the husband could lead with confidence, and the wife could trust in his leadership. Trust is not easily obtained; it needs to be developed, especially with those who have been deeply hurt.

Now, this man and his wife were not going to take any chances; they prayed daily for the Lord to keep their words encouraged toward each other. They decided to undergo some Christian counseling in order to learn where their breakdown had occurred so that it did not happen again.

The Storyteller Collection

They had their pastor remarry them in a ceremony just for them and the Lord. You see, this was not for the masses; this was to hear the verbal vows they had said to each other once again.

Each day, they would focus on what they could do to build each other up. And Mary had been right; the wife would become a mother. They decided to adopt.

End

The Storyteller Collection

The Storyteller Collection

The Storyteller Collection

The Storyteller Collection

The Relative

Of whom the whole family in heaven and earth is named...
Ephesians 3:15

This is dedicated to those who desire to leave their old stories behind and begin again.

She sends you salutations. She realizes that you won't know her name, so giving it would be superfluous. But she is confident that you do know of one of her ancestors. You see, one of her forefathers was known as a man of incredible endurance. Her forefather was known by only one name: Job.

When she was in her "dim" era, she would say to everyone, "I am a descendant of King David!" You see, she wanted to be affiliated with the likes of David, because David had God's own heart, not to mention that David was a king.

In his youth, he had come from humble beginnings, as she had, but as a king, he was wealthy and had fine children. He was quite privileged; as a man, there was nothing he wanted that was out of his reach.

He eventually met and married the love of his life, Bathsheba, even though he had to kill her husband to make it happen.

But what was most important was that David was truly sorrowful and tried to make amends when it was brought to his attention that, by doing this deed, he had sinned against God.

Now, David knew how to pray to get God's attention. He prayed so sincerely and humbly that, though he was indeed punished through the death of their first child, because his heart was right, God forgave him. David was also the father of another great man, Solomon, who was known far and wide for his wisdom. Yes, David was favored by God. He was a king of great wealth, he had the love of his life by his side, and he was the father of the great king Solomon. Yes, she wanted to be part of that family. But alas, it was not meant to be.

You see, she found out later, in her clarity, that she was actually related to Job! Now, who the heck wanted to be in that family? Who wanted to be related to that man? Do you remember what happened to him?

If not, then let me give you a little recap of the life and times of Job, taken from the book of Job: Job lived in the land of Uz.

The Storyteller Collection

He was known a righteous man who loved the Lord unquestionably and turned away from sin. For this, the Lord blessed him greatly for his love and loyalty.

Job had many sons and daughters. He had vast lands and stock. At one time, he had everything a man would want, and he was regaled as one of greatest men in his realm, but he was no king.

The Lord was very proud of Job, and He would let it be known. However, Satan felt that if Job had not had all that the Lord had bestowed upon him, he would curse God. So God suffered it to be so and put Job in Satan's hands. When this happened, Job had everything, and then it was all taken away in a most horrendous way. Finally, his very own body was afflicted. He wife was done with him and told him to curse God and die! (This story can be found in Job 2:9).

His friends tried to reason with Job that, somehow, he had done something unforgivable in the sight of God, and they stated they would pray for him—after he was gone. All of this made Job question why he had ever even been born!

When she had first realized this, she screamed, "This can't be true!" She had no desire to be related to a man like that. She didn't have his fortitude or his endurance; when she broke a nail, she was apt to call the suicide prevention line!

But, as you know, one can pick one's friends but not one's relatives. It was so sad to say that she was a direct descendant of her forefather, Job. Sigh.

Before Her Time Began...

God once again had a conversation with Satan; this time, it was about her. When she had not yet been conceived in her mother's womb, God was holding her close and whispering into her ear.

You see, God knew she was going to be a little girl before her conception. Of course, He would know this; He's God—He created her. He also knew that she would have a love for Him, like her ancestor did, that was unfathomable. So imagine this conversation He had with Satan about her:

"Do you know whom I am carrying in my arms?" God said to him. "It's Job's granddaughter! Though she has not been conceived yet, she has a love for me that is unparalleled. I can feel it in her little spirit."

"And this interests me how?" said Satan. "You are just going to make her life lovely and pleasant, and You will spoil her incessantly. She will be born into one of the best homes and given the best of opportunities. She'll marry the perfect husband and have little perfect children, all because she's related to Job."

"So, you think I should put her destiny in your hands so that you can treat her like you did my servant Job?"

"His whole family line has been protected by you. Put some obstacles in her way as she is growing up, and watch how she turns out. Then, see how much she exalts you through the years. Job cried out for what he had known and then lost. How would she be if she had never known these things in the first place?"

So, in a wisdom that few could understand, God gave Job's descendant over to the perils of Satan. As God handed her over to Satan, He warned him, "You can change her destiny, but you cannot kill her!"

Parentage

Satan smiled devilishly as he whisked away with Job's descendant. He had big plans for her, he dared say. The first thing he did was change her parentage. Oh, yes. He implanted her into a particular woman whose lineage dated back to that of Gomer. Now, I know you remember Gomer, the daughter of Diblaim. She was the harlot whom Hosea married, of all people!

This descendant of Gomer was just like her ancestor; she was brought up a spoiled only child who got away with everything.

The Storyteller Collection

She had her first child when she was twelve; however, the child did not live.

The next year, she was caught stealing and robbing and was sent away to prison. She came out of that institution no better off. She went on to have many children.

She was impregnated a total of sixteen times, by different men. Her education in prison just taught her how to be a better criminal.

Job's descendent was the fourth child born live to Gomer's descendant. Understand that Satan didn't just have her born to a woman who should have never had a single child; she was born out of a sex act with the child's father. She was having sex for money when she was impregnated!

You see, her birth father was full of years, and her birth mother at the time was not. So does one honestly believe this was a union of love? Of course not. Gomer's descendent had a boyfriend when she was seeing the child's father. When she found out she was pregnant, like a Maury Povich plot, she told the boyfriend that it was his baby. Of course, when the child was born, she looked so much like her real father that there was no denying it.

But like her ancestor, Gomer, she gave the child her boyfriend's last name anyway.

The Storyteller Collection

What a beginning in life! Satan had pulled a fast one on God—or so he thought.

The Life of a Trick Baby

Well, there she was. This was the child's beginning; she had a jailbird for a mother and a senior citizen for a father. Now, her birth father was not your typical senior citizen. He told her once that she kept him young. His line dated back to that of Esau, Jacob's older brother. Like Esau, he was strong and single-minded.

He was a protector of what was his, and he would fight tooth and nail for it. He had but one character flaw, like his forefather: when things were complicated, he took the path of least resistance. Like his forefather, Esau, when situations challenged him, he felt that the birthright of his child was not as important as his appetites. The child's birth father felt that it was easier to relent than to fight for his child's birthright. Also like his forefather, he was a good man, but he was not a great man.

If that wasn't bad enough, her birth mother had no feelings for her whatsoever. This child was known (not-so-secretly) as a "trick baby"; yet, eventually, trick babies do grow up.

The child's only value to her birth mother was that of additional income.

You see, her birth mother was constantly giving her away to her friends and old acquaintances. She had been fostered in so many homes that she had lost count. She was even sent to a state facility a couple of times.

Job's granddaughter remembered that when she was very young, she loved to go to church. She didn't know that this wasn't the norm for a child of that young age, but by the age of seven, she would get herself and her little sister dressed, and they walked about ten blocks to church. Why she did this she didn't understand.

Her birth mother was not a religious woman, and neither was her birth father. She had never gone to church with either of them, yet she had had this desire to go to church ever since she could remember. Since she knew her birth mother would never take her, she decided she would take herself and her baby sister, too.

At a young age, she loved to hear the music in church. She remembered each time she would stay until the music was over; then, she would just go to the next church down the block to hear more music.

Once, she was stopped from leaving after the music was over.

The Storyteller Collection

The pastor, thinking that she and her sister belonged to someone in the church, made them sit there until church services had concluded.

She remembered that when she was eleven, she started one of her foster mothers on the path to attending a local church, to which her foster mother belonged for more than thirty years until her death.

She didn't know what drew her to church, but it was something she had an innate desire to do. As she was growing up, she always felt that she did not belong in her loveless family (with the exception of her father, of course). She never felt a part of things; she always felt like she was on the outside, looking in. She hated each time she was sent back to her mother's house. It was so filthy and unkempt.

On one of the rare occasions when she was sent home, her mother was living in a one-bedroom duplex with her husband, her oldest daughter, her brother-in-law, her little sister, three baby brothers, and her two oldest brothers. Her youngest brother had been living with her mother's best friend for quite a while at the time.

Imagine ten people in a one-bedroom duplex. They didn't even have room for her there. Her oldest brother was sleeping in the bathtub!

She didn't want to stay, and she didn't stay long, which was also the norm.

When she was eleven, she was in the foster home of some nice people. She could still remember this so clearly because they had some friends who were childless. They had been so nice to her, and she had decided she wanted them to adopt her.
The little eleven-year-old prayed the first prayer she had every prayed in her life that night. She remembered it succinctly: "Dear God, I promise I will be a good little girl if you will give me a mommy and daddy."

The next day, she proceeded to ask the couple to adopt her! She thought things were as simple as that when it came to praying, but it wasn't. It was so sad; the couple had no desire to adopt anyone, and she felt so rejected. This was the first time she had ever felt the pain of rejection. All the things that had happened to her before were things she was used to, but she wasn't used to this. She remembered that this was the first time she had put pen to paper and had begun to write her feelings out.

Well, time marched on, and even though she has no desire to go through all her life's struggles, she just want people to know that it wasn't good. The last time she had lived with her birth mother, she had been twelve.

How ironic; that was almost the same age that Gomer had last lived with her mother.

Each time she would think her life was getting better, it then felt like God would throw a curveball and ruin everything. One spring, many years ago, her second son had been accidently smothered to death, and the pain was horrific.

She had never known that level of pain before. The loss of a child is akin to ripping your very soul apart with rusty gardening shears. The pain was so acute that it felt as though, with each breath, the shears would thrust in deeper, with no relenting. It nearly destroyed her. It did destroy her marriage. She prayed to God that He would never visit pain like that on her again. And He didn't; as time passed, she was blessed with more children.

To sum up her life in a nutshell, her husband decided that he didn't want to be a husband or a father anymore, and he left. She had to raise her children on her own. She had her youngest child stolen from her by one of his paternal family members, and it took more than two years for her to finally get him back.

Five years later, after the child had been found, he was having irrational and emotional problems, and she started taking him to counseling.

One day, the counselor told her she had to give him back, because he thought she had stolen him away from his real parents!

She had thought the counselor was crazy. He didn't realize how long it had taken and how hard it had been for her to find him and get him back. He told her it wasn't about her; it was for the sake of the child. After a year of refusals, she finally relented. It didn't matter what she wanted or what those people had done to her; it was all about what the child felt. In hindsight, she finally realized she should have gone to a different counselor.

Everything that could go wrong in her life did go wrong, and at several points in her life, she truly considered committing suicide just so she didn't have to hurt anymore. The only thing that would stop her was the question of who would care for her children.

She had a fear that they would end up in foster care like she had, with no one wanting or loving them. That was what kept her from the brink of total despair. She wondered who could have this much bad luck in her life. Why did God hate her so? Was she so unlovable that He couldn't bear to hear her cries?

She was not educated in those early years, and she very much wanted to go back to school, but each time she would set up a sitter and start classes, she would have to cancel. This happened so often she screamed, "I will never try to go to school again!" However, as soon as she could obtain a new sitter, there she was, knocking on the door of higher learning and asking if she could come in.

With so much responsibility on her for such a long time (she also helped raise her birth mother's youngest children when she died), she took solace in eating. She had been overweight for more than thirty years. Over those years, she felt unloved, unwanted, fat, and broke.

There would be times when she just couldn't even talk about God. She would go to church, but she wouldn't talk to Him. She had said she didn't believe in Him anymore but went back to church anyway. She had yelled out in anger and pain at Him, but later, she would still be seeking His face. She knew that there were two things in her life that meant a great deal to her: her love of Jesus Christ and her writing. There was nothing else in her life she felt she had.

There was also no relationship between her siblings and herself as they grew into adulthood. They were not taught to respect one another or to maintain a relationship of mutual respect, so they didn't.

What did she do to deserve a life like this? She thought, "There has to be an answer to all of this; there just hast to be." There was, and it was called restoration.

Restoration

Even with all the things that had happened to her in life, Satan could not get her to stop loving the Lord. She had no love for herself at times, but she had love for the Lord.

Through the years, unbeknownst to her when she was quite young, she would write poetry to and about God. She would let Him know through her writings how much she loved Him and what He meant to the innermost part of her.

Even though she was born to a woman who didn't love or want her, she still loved Him. Even though her mother had fostered and given her away to people she didn't often know, she still loved Him. Even though He did not give her adoptive parents, she still loved Him. Even when her child died and her pain was oppressively severe, she still loved Him.

Even when her husband left her and she had to live life alone, she still loved Him. Even when she had to give her youngest child back to his captors, she still loved Him. Even when she could not obtain congruent education, she still loved Him.

Even when she was attacked and beaten, she still called to Him by His name.

She didn't understand why He had picked her for all this grief, but she still loved Him and, for the love of Him, she would stand on His word for the rest of her life.

One day, she began to read the thirty-seventh chapter of the book of Ezekiel.

As she read, she found that Ezekiel, one day, was carried out in the Spirit and sat down in a valley full of bones. As he looked, there were many, and they were very dry. The Lord asked him if those dry bones could live again. He said to the Lord, "Only you know that, Lord." The Lord was trying to teach him a great lesson and said, "Son of man, prophesize over these bones in my name. Breathe life into these bones, according to the name of the Lord."

Ezekiel did as he was told, and the bones became alive again. Skin grew over the bones, and, finally, he prophesized that breath be instilled in them. These bones became living human beings again.

She then thought of her own life; could she breathe life into her meager existence? Could she find a new hope, a new beginning, a new joy for her wanting existence?

The Storyteller Collection

She, too, started prophesying over herself. She breathed new life into her being. She wrote a new life story for herself, this time with a different ending.

She spoke peace and happiness into her life. She spoke wealth and value into her being. She spoke life's passion into her senses. She spoke love into her heart. She spoke financial abundance into her purse. And she spoke perfect health into her body. She spoke these prophesies over herself, in the name of the Jesus Christ.

She accepted the fact of being in the family of Job, but she was no longer going to cry out to the Lord, "Why me?" She was going to thank Him for her story—a story that He wanted her to share with all who had similar experiences.

Without her experiences, she would have no story to tell. She would have no way to show others the way out of it. This was not only her story; this was "our" story. This was about our mothers, our fathers, our dead children. This was about our pain, our loss, our challenges. But through it all, this was about our restoration as well.

End

The Storyteller Collection

Epilogue

As the woman slept, Satan was once again in the presence of God. It had only been a drop of time in eternity since last they had spoken of her, yet many years had gone by in that time. "So, you did your worst with the life of Job's granddaughter, and she still loves me. You took her birthright, you took her happiness, and you took her hope and her future, yet she still stands."

"I don't see how that could have happened," snorted Satan. "I have crumbled people with far less effort. It must've been you!" Satan accused. "You did something to her, didn't You? What was it that You whispered in her ear before You gave her to me?"

"I gave her assurances, as any father would. I told her to fear not, for I would restore what would be taken from her. I told her I would restore the years that the locust and the cankerworm and the caterpillar would take from her." This promise was found in Joel 2:25.

"I assured her that she would be given a new story and a new happy ending, and that she would share it with the world. My promise was that, whatever was taken, I would restore that which was lost."

The Storyteller Collection

Lineage

Let me clarify the references of people in the Bible to whom I believe we are all related:

The life and times of Job can be found in the book of Job. Job was known far and wide as a respectful, generous, and noble man. Though his children were not as good in spirit, Job remained true to God and turned away from sin. Job was challenged with everything that could happen to one man. Once he was healthy and wealthy, and he had many children.

He lost all of this, and though it's not said how long over the course of his life these tragedies continued, it is safe to say they did happen over some length of time. Year after year, as these trials and tribulations ensconced his life, he would not relinquish his love for God. He is known as the man who "endured."

Gomer was the wife of Hosea, a truly righteous man. Gomer's life is detailed in the book of Hosea. Hosea (which means "salvation") was the son of Beeri, a prophet in Israel in the eighth century BC, and he authored the book of prophecies bearing his name. He was one of the twelve prophets of the Jewish Hebrew Bible. Hosea is often seen as the "prophet of doom," but underneath his message of destruction is a promise of restoration.

The Storyteller Collection

According to the book of Hosea, he married the prostitute Gomer, the daughter of Diblaim, at God's command. Hosea's family life reflected the relationship between God and Israel. Even though Gomer ran away from Hosea and slept with other men, he loved her anyway and forgave her. Likewise, even though the people of Israel worshipped other gods, God continued to love them and did not abandon His covenant with them.

Esau is the eldest son of Isaac. In Genesis, Esau's birth is noted as such. Though they were fraternal twins, Jacob was born after Esau, which made Esau the eldest. Esau was a man of integrity, but he was weak. He thought so little of his birthright that he sold it to his brother for a bowl of stew. Later, when Jacob tricked Esau out of his birthright blessing from their father, he became angry and vengeful.

My question has always been this: why? He sold his birthright to Jacob initially to satisfy his appetite, so it stands to reason that Jacob stole nothing from Esau; he just took what he had bartered for in the first place. This is why I envision Esau as a good man but not a great one.

The Storyteller Collection

The Storyteller Collection

Marie Browders'
The Storyteller©

Seeking Justice

Seeking Justice

The journey had been long but well worth it, for she was resolved to seek out *his* help. When she arrived at his court, the first thing she noticed was the crowds. Many had come, seeking his wisdom for their issues.

She had traveled a long way, and she, too, wanted to be heard. As she threaded her way through the crowds of people, who were a variety of sizes and shapes, she managed to get a sliver of a look of him, even though she was still two feet deep in the back. She finally gazed upon this wise man.

He looked as others had described him to her: tall and adorned in rich red robes trimmed with gold. An austere crown graced his head just above his brow; it was ensconced with emeralds and rubies. His hair was wavy and brown. His beard was brown also; however, it was laced with streaks of gray, as his time on earth had been long by the time she sought him out. His clear brown eyes, the shape of his brows, and his square chin gave her the assurance that he was the man she sought:

The Storyteller Collection

King Solomon, the wisest of all men who ever lived on earth. Many crowded around him, waiting with bated breath as he extended his brand of wisdom to them.

To see and hear him speak was amazing. He would listen intently to whoever was speaking to him; he did not interrupt those who were pleading their cases. His wisdom was so infinite that no one would question it. When he had been a young man, God had wanted to give him a gift; instead of riches, fame, and glory, Solomon had asked for wisdom. God had given him not only an abundance of wisdom but He also blessed him liberally with discerning and understanding. God had enlarged the depth of Solomon's heart as well, to keep him humble. Over the years, Solomon became known as the wisest and wealthiest man in the entire world.

The woman thought, "Yes, he is who I want to plead my case in front of." She began again to try to make her way up front.

King Solomon noticed her pushing her way through the crowd, and, in his wisdom, he could tell that she was not from his time. As some people tried to stop her from getting through, King Solomon motioned to them to let her be.

In front of the good king himself now and knowing the customs of this time, she bowed before him.

The Storyteller Collection

He nodded with pleasure at her respect.

"Rise, Daughter." He motioned. "I see that you've journeyed a long way. Who are you, and why have you come?"

"Sire," she beseeched him, "I am no one significant, just a woman from another time. But I request that I be heard."

"Well, speak then. What do you seek from me?"
"My lord king Solomon, I seek justice!"

"I see that you've traveled far, down through the ages, to seek this justice from me. But why?"

"In my time, you are still revered as the wisest man ever born. There is no one in my time who would give me the level of justice I seek from you. In my courts, there is a thing called 'no fault,' and, therefore, there is no justice. I came here because true justice is what I seek."

"But why did you come all this way?" inquired the king. "Why didn't you take your plight to our Lord and Savior, Jesus?"

"I love Jesus like no other, Sire," she explained. "But Jesus is known far and wide for His forgiveness. I feel that He would just forgive the one I seek justice against. I don't want him forgiven; I want justice!"

"Well then, what of Paul, a man of true integrity? Why not seek out his counsel?"

"I agree, Sire," she acknowledged. "Paul, with the help of our Lord and Savior, has changed every area of his life. But his is one of great sacrifice; I will sacrifice no longer. Sire, give me justice!"

"Well maybe a woman would be best. How about our beloved Esther? No kinder woman can be found."

"I did first think of Queen Esther, I'll admit, Sire," conceded the woman. "She would not speak of sacrifice; she would counsel me on endurance. Sire, I have endured this pain and loss long enough. I want justice that only you can deliver."

"Have you entertained the thought of our first mother, Eve? She has been here since time began. She has insight into matters such as yours."

"Yes, and I love her because she was the first woman; she is the embodiment of all womanhood. But she is still ashamed of her actions back in the garden, and she is constantly trying to make amends for it. I will no longer feel shame for my actions; justice is what I seek now."

There was a great deal of mumbling in understanding of what she cried out for. They, too, sought their own brands of justice.

The Storyteller Collection

"In my time, people still talk of the wisdom you showed to the baby and the two mothers. They speak about how God had tapped you to build His temple. As much as He loved your father, He would not let him build it because he was a warring king.

"He chose you to resurrect His sanctuary because of your wisdom and understanding. That is why I chose you for my plight."

"Well, well," said King Solomon, leaning back and scratching his beard. "I must say, you are persistent."

For a moment, he looked on her intently and then waved to the crowd. "Court is adjourned for today." The king dismissed everyone. "She has traveled far to seek my help. I will take private counsel with her."

There was noise from the back, as someone pushed through. A short, round man with a well-worn tunic of gray draped around his shoulder spoke up. He looked anxious as he boldly said, "Sire, hear me, please! I am a humble farmer, and I, too, have traveled far to seek your counsel. Three days I have traveled for my justice, as well. My neighbor and I had a dispute over a well; we both sought ownership. The city magistrate ruled in my favor, which pleased me greatly.

The Storyteller Collection

My neighbor was angry, and, in the darkness of night, he poisoned my well. The next day, when I watered some of my stock, they fell dead. Sire that could have been my children who drank from that well. The magistrate stated this must be taken to the good king Solomon."

The king walked over to him and put his hand on his shoulder in compassion. "My good man, you are owed a measure of justice, and it will be done. But allow me to counsel this daughter, as her travels are much greater than yours." The farmer bowed with relief and agreed.

King Solomon turned, and all bowed before him as he said, "Let's walk the gardens. There, you will tell me your story, and I will do my best to give you all you seek."

The woman was relieved that he would give her an audience and was willing to listen to her plight. She followed him closely out into the garden, and then he motioned her to walk next to him.

"Thank you for hearing me out."
"Daughter, you had to travel this far back in time; your plight must be great."
"It is, Sire."

"I'm listening. Tell me your story."

"I was once a married woman, Sire, but no more. The man I married took all that I had to offer, mentally, physically, emotionally, and financially. He took all I had until I had no more to give. Once he found that I could give no more, I was of no use to him then."

"I see," the king said, as he continued to stroll the gardens with her.

"Sire, my pain is great over this, as I am no longer a young woman who can begin again. I fear to trust or believe in another again. Others still held him in high esteem, and I feel that I am thrown by the wayside. Pain is now my only companion. Sire, I have tried to let it go and go on with my life, but, deep in my anger and pain, I feel that he must pay for his insurrection toward me. I feel that, if I receive no justice, I am not long for this world, as I cannot take this pain of injustice any longer."

There was silence for a bit as they strolled one of the most beautiful gardens she had ever seen, with rows and rows of daffodils, hyacinths, and daisies spread far and wide. There were well-manicured roses lined perfectly around the green shrubbery, complementing it beautifully. The shrubbery looked like a sculptured work of art.

"So, take me back to the beginning.

Prior to marriage, what did this imbecile offer you to lure you into his marriage trap?"

"Well…uh…" She hesitated. "Nothing actually, Sire. In those earlier days, he just promised that he would pay his part."

"And did he keep this unwritten contract?"
"No, King." She was firm about this. "He did not!"

"The knave!" the king echoed. "And did you immediately throw him in the streets, like the dog he was?"

"Uh…er…" she stammered. "No."
"No?" repeated the king. "I see."
"Sire, you see, in the beginning, I thought that things would eventually get better."
"Tell me of the rubies and diamonds he showered you with to keep you from requesting a bill of divorcement?"

"I was never showered with anything during the marriage."

"So, he offered nothing to you for the privilege of marriage and to share your bed?"
The woman shook her head, blushing at what the king had so intimately said.
"Then, what of the marriage bed itself? Did he share intimate delights with you to a level that covered all his other shortcomings?"

"I am embarrassed to say no, Sire." She bowed her head. "The experience left me wanting. It would have been easier if he would have desired to be intimate with me, but I always felt that, in his mind, he belonged to another whom he could never have. He once told me to be content with what I had, for he had nothing else to offer me."

"Well," the king rubbed his beard, thinking. "It appeared that he was aware of what he had to offer during the life of the marriage."

Warm tears sprouted to her eyes. Once again, she was reminded how little she had received from the man she married.

"How long did this union last?"

"We were together a total of six years."

King Solomon once again fell into silence, until they came upon a shaded table made of large planks of wood that were polished to a mirrored glaze.

"Come, sit with me. Let's share refreshment." The king offered her a seat.

One of his servants immediately appeared, and, upon the king's instructions, poured but one goblet of wine.

"Here," the king said. "Share mine with me."

The woman thought his gesture was nice but couldn't understand why he didn't just have his servant pour two goblets.

The Storyteller Collection

She thought, "Maybe it's a custom here, but he is a king, and I cannot partake before him."

"Sire, please." She humbled herself. "You refresh yourself first, and I will take what is left." The king took the goblet back and smiled knowingly.

"Before I render my decision to your plight, I have a lesson to teach you.

"I offered you my cup with all that I had in it. You refused, seeking me to refresh myself first. When one gives all that one has to offer to someone, he or she runs the risk of that that individual will take it all. These people are called 'takers.' They are selfish and narrow-minded. If they return your cup back empty, most will have the audacity to ask you for more. They feel that, since you offered it, they can take as much as they want. These people don't have your best interests at heart; they will always leave you without.

"On the other side, there are those who are called 'givers.' You would not refresh yourself until I had gone first. You are a giver. You think of your neighbor before you do yourself. You are a caring and loving individual who will always treat others more kindly than you will treat yourself. Takers and givers are unequally yoked. Of the two, there will always be one who will be left wanting. There is the one who gives so much that it makes the taker actually lose respect for his giving partner.

And, of course, there is the taker who will drain the life out of a giver until the giver will wither on the vine.

"Not all are at these extremes, for these are at the very far ends of the scale. There are those who are 'sharers.' They believe in equal balance. When they seek to be in relationships, they will pour portions from their jug to share, being mindful of what is shared with them. If they see that all is taken from the cup they shared, and another does not offer to refill it, a sharer will know that person is not for him or her. If the sharer allows this pattern to continue, the sharer will end up becoming a giver, giving until it hurts, with no one giving to the sharer in return. The sharer spends no more time on this taker, as it would be a waste of time; the sharer's needs will never be met in a relationship such as this.

"A sharer is also balanced enough recognize a giver's character flaw. A sharer knows that a giver would try to out give God! The giver is trying to obligate people to himself or herself with all that giving. These types of people will complain to others how they gave and did not receive as much as they had given.

"A taker's nature is always to take what is offered and not to share. A giver gives too much and won't allow others to share with him or her.

A sharer is looking for a balance that would benefit both in the relationship—equally. That is why the Father speaks of being 'equally yoked.'"

"You must understand that an extreme Giver and an extreme Taker will never live happily ever after. The Taker, just like the Giver, has a character flaw because just like the Giver will always give too much, Taker will always take too much. The Giver so wants someone to love and care for them that they will give all that they have and starve themselves to death."

She couldn't believe that he had taught her such a valuable lesson with a simple cup of wine. But this all made sense to her.

"But you came for justice and I chose to teach you a valuable lesson. So now I will speak of the justice you so diligently seek."

The king squared his shoulders and leaned forward cupping her hands in his and said, "I find *you* guilty of this injustice you seek."

"It took me less than five minutes to conclude that the relationship would have never worked. You chose to invest six entire years expecting it to get better and you allowed your Taker to take all that you had without offering anything in return."

"When this imbecile did not offer you little trinkets and treasures to lure you into marriage; but took from you with no compulsion, he revealed the character of an extremist, a Taker."

"When soon after the relationship began, he easily broke his covenant with you of paying his part to the debt collector and you gave him no penalty for his actions, you had done an injustice to him by allowing him not to be accountable and an injustice to yourself by continuing to devalue your worth in the eyes of that knave. You are a classic Giver."

"But Sire," She beseeched him, "I did no harm to him, why would I be the blame?"

"Here me as I speak, Daughter," commanded the king. "I found lacking in the relationship within five minutes time, so did you."

"However, you chose to continue in this charade hoping eventually you would be able to pick up milk with a fork. When you did not make him accountable for his actions, the fault fell on your shoulders."

"Daughter," The king let go of her hands and straightened up, "You're not angry at him as much as you're angry and disappointed at yourself for not choosing wisely."

The Storyteller Collection

"Sire then what can I do now? Will I forever be a Giver and never a Sharer? How can I go on with my life?"

"You traveled over time to obtain justice. You came seeking the truth and you found it. You were fearless in your quest. You were not disappointed as you sought justice not retribution. Your time is now waiting for your return. Your friends and family wait with loving kindness to welcome you back home."

"As you journey back, I suggest you stop and visit Hosea; he married the harlot Gomer, remember? She is a classic taker. Let him share his story with you.

"Sit and take bread on your way back with John the Baptist. Listen to the story of how he did everything right and the whim of a woman (Herodias) got him beheaded; she was also a Taker.

"They will share their wisdom on this subject and assist you in putting your life back into perspective. You will then recognize the next taker who seeks your attention. In time, you will heal your self-inflicted wounds."

The king stood and embraced her as he walked side by side with her, leading her toward one of the great gates leading out of the palace.

"Sire," She sought his advice one last time before she left. "What am I to do with my anger and pain inside me, for it is still great? How am I to make it through?"

"Daughter, have no fear of that." He smiled generously. "Did I forget to mention that Jesus awaits you also in your time? You sought justice here. Seek forgiveness there, with Him."

End

The Storyteller Collection

Marie Browders'
The Storyteller©

The Seven

The Storyteller Collection

The Storyteller Collection

...seven men of good repute full of the Spirit and of wisdom...

The Seven

Prologue

"You summoned me, Moses?" Simon Peter asked, as he approached him.

"Yes." Moses motioned him over. "Today, I had an audience with our Lord and Savior, Jesus. He suggested that we take a trip to earth and meet with group of young men."

"Earthly young men?" Simon Peter queried. "Whatever for?"

"Our Lord and Savior has not given up on these children, as He never gave up on us. He would like seven of us to go down and tell our stories to them."

The Storyteller Collection

"But that feels so useless." Simon Peter shook his head. "Our Lord has tried for centuries to have them turn from their wicked ways. He showed them again and again the way to everlasting life, and only a few chose to follow Him. What can we do that He has not done?"

"We can share our life's stories," Moses stated. "We will not preach or teach. We will not try to inflict fear in them. Our Lord never did that. We will simply share our stories. This is all we have to give them: our lives, our experiences, our shortcomings and failures, and our triumphs. We will let them know about us."

"Interesting..." Simon Peter rubbed his beard. "That, we can do."

"You mentioned that we will be seven," Simon Peter asked. "Which seven do you have in mind?"
"I have given this a lot of thought." Moses turned and seated himself in his oversized wooden chair. "I think it should be you, Simon Peter, and me. I have been thinking of Jacob and Joseph, for they have great stories to tell."

"Well, what of King David?" suggested Simon Peter. "Wouldn't his life be of great significance?"
"I agree with you that King David's life is something to be told, but, like our Lord and Savior, he is bigger than life. I feel that these young men would relate more to his son Amnon, don't you think?"

The Storyteller Collection

"Well, if you choose Amnon, you must include his brother Absalom. But I suggest that you keep these two far apart from each other."

"I have to agree with you." Moses nodded.
"So, how many do we have now?" Moses asked.
Simon Peter counted: "Myself, you, Jacob, Joseph, Amnon, and Absalom. We need one more."
"How about the Apostle Paul?" Moses recommended. "He was a heinous individual who turned his life around to be one of the Lord's greatest apostles."

"I agree, Moses," Simon Peter said. "We now have our seven."
"When should we depart?"
"We seven must pray and wait on the Lord," Moses stated. "He will direct our path."

Earth

Two young men had eyed a flier that was posted out of their social economics class on the door.
"A seminar—for men only?" read the first young man, who was a bit taller and fuller than the second young man. He played on the basketball team. "No chicks? Count me out." The second young man was shorter, and he sported a close beard; his first. He was on the track-and-field team.

"You do know that, if we attend, we get an automatic A in social economics," said the second young man, as he continued to read down the flier.

"And it's only for one day. We also get to go home as soon it's over. For a free afternoon and an automatic A, I'll go."

"Yeah, I guess I can hang, too for a day, chicks or no chicks," agreed the first young man, after giving it some thought. However, as he read further, he commented, "But there's a hitch: it is mandatory that we bring another guy with us. Who could we bring?"

"The flier states that you can bring any guy of any age, so bring your brother or your cousin," suggested the second young man. "I think I will bring my neighbor; he owes me."

"So, I wonder what this is all about?" asked the first young man. "I mean, it does not state on the flier, and the professor did not say; it just says that you will know the topic tomorrow morning when you get there. Oh, look at the top of the flier; it says 'The Seven.' I wonder what that means..."

"Who cares?" the second young man said. "I can sit through anything if I get an automatic A for a class and get the rest of the day off."

"Well, I guess you're right," the first young man agreed. "It's probably a talk about people around the world or something."

Changing the subject, the first young man lowered his voice.

"I heard you got a certain girl knocked up."
"Did I?" The second young man smiled. "Well, she has got to prove it first. If she gave it up to me, she could have given it to someone else."

"Wasn't she a virgin, though?" the first young man countered.

"Was she?" His friend smiled again. "How was I supposed to know? I was only in her pants once. It wasn't like she was my girl. I believe that if she'd give it to me, she would give it to anyone."
"Man, you are cold." The first young man shook his head.

"No," he corrected his friend, "I'm a realist. Besides, all these girls are b———."
"Come on," the first young man said. "Let's go and get a couple of cold ones."

The Seminar

"Okay, settle down, settle down." The professor shushed them. "The sooner we get started, the sooner you will be allowed to leave. Make sure everyone has signed in. We have a different kind of seminar for you today. As you can see, there are seven men on stage. They have traveled very far to speak to you today.

"I will let our guest speakers introduce themselves and let you know who will be speaking first. Please give them your undivided attention, as they are not doing this for monetary compensation.

They are here simply to share their stories."
Moses arose and motioned Simon Peter to start things off.

Simon Peter looked at the unruly young men and shook his head. "Father, are you sure about all of this?" he silently prayed. "I will do this for Your honor and glory."

The first thing he was aware of was the giggles, as they pointed to his clothes. One laughed out loud and stated that this must be a costume seminar. He was not surprised; if they could disrespect our Lord and Savior, who was he to expect anything else?

Simon Peter walked to the podium. His youth had long since gone, and his hair was filled with silvery gray, as was his beard. His face was etched with many lines of the wisdom he had earned through time. Simon Peter, in fact, had been known in his youth as the "prince of all the apostles."

Even in his old age, his gait was direct, with purpose. His wrinkled hands surrounded the edges of the podium; he cleared his throat and began his story.

The Storyteller Collection

Simon Peter's Story
Forgiving Oneself

"Gentleman," he began, "I am Simon Peter, son of Jonah and one of Jesus' original twelve disciples. All my life, I was just a humble fisherman. I had done well at my chosen career. I thought that I would live and die a fisherman, until one day, my brother, Andrew, came to me with some exciting news. You see, he had been a disciple of Jesus' cousin, John the Baptist. But once he had heard John the Baptist speak of Jesus as the true 'Messiah,' he was beside himself in his excitement.

"My brother brought him to me, requesting that I meet Him. Now, I had always been a godly man from the time I was a child, but I have to tell you that I was not overly impressed at first. My brother and I were fishermen, and the fishing had not been good for a while. Though preoccupied, I obediently bowed to Him but kept on toward my fishing boat, as I had a wife to care for and a mother-in-law who was in poor health.

"Since I had not caught anything for days, I was preoccupied with this. I paid no notice to the fact that Jesus had come up to my boat. I asked how could I help Him, and He requested that I put my nets in the water again.

I explained to Him that that day was not a good day for fishing. He requested that I do it again, so to appease Him, I threw my nets into the water again, noticing that He touched the water. I couldn't believe it; there was such a large catch that I required His help to pull them into the boat. "I looked at him and asked, 'What do you want of me, Messiah?' He simply said, 'Come, and I will make you a fisher of men.'

"That was the moment that my whole life changed. I had thought I had been content with my life. At thirty-five years old, I had a good wife, I lived in a nice house, and I was in the same business as my father, Jonah, before me and his father before him. But all of that meant nothing when this Christ asked me to follow Him; my life changed in an instant."

"I have to admit, I enjoyed traveling around and speaking beside Jesus. We traveled to many cities and townships, and I saw firsthand that He healed the sick and fed the many. He was so gentle when speaking to people that they fell in love with Him without trying. He taught us about loving our fellow man. He spoke a lot in parables. He wanted us to take His teachings in and glean the embedded lessons out of them. Wherever we went, people bowed to the twelve of us as well, and, in all honesty, I liked being honored just for being in His presence.

"Little did I know that He would be gone soon, and we would have to carry on with His Word. My life changed once again at what was to be known as the Last Supper. There, Jesus stated that He would be betrayed by one of us that night. We couldn't think of who would betray Him. We twelve were all so close. For some time now, we had been traveling all over with Him; who would want to betray Him? I jumped to my feet, and I told Him that it would not be me! He then looked at me and smiled sadly, saying that, before the cock crowed three times, I would deny Him. Even after all this time, I can still see the sad look on His face when He said those words to me."

"Later that night, it was as He said; He was arrested, and I was questioned as to whether I had any affiliation with Him. Three times, I said no."

"Imagine denying someone you loved so deeply. After He was hanged on a cross, I wept bitterly and begged for forgiveness. I saw Him one last time, and He smiled and said that He had already forgiven me. But try as I might, I could not seem to forgive myself. The one who actually betrayed Him the night of the Last Supper was Judas for thirty pieces of gold. Later that night, he hanged himself.

"After Christ's death, the rest of us traveled far and wide, teaching His Word. As time passed, each one of us was killed for our beliefs.

I was the last. As I was about to be put to death on a cross, as was the custom in those days, I asked to be hung upside down, as I felt I was not worthy to be hanged as our Lord and Savior had been.

"From the beginning, I was fiercely loyal to Jesus. Like the other apostles, I left the life I knew, to follow Jesus for three years. He taught all of us about the kingdom of heaven and blessed us to be filled with His Holy Spirit. Because of my aggressiveness, I was made the lead speaker for the twelve of us."

"Often, I would speak before I thought, which at times led me to embarrassment. But I wanted others to know how much I loved Him and that I would do anything for Him. Sometimes, I would let my passions rule my head instead of my faith in God. But Jesus generously forgave me, time after time. As you can see, by asking to be hanged upside down at the end of my life, I had not forgiven myself."

"Sometimes, the things we have done may feel so heinous that we think we could never be forgiven, but that is incorrect. I now live with Jesus, in eternity. He has taught me how to forgive myself. I praise and honor Him for this."

As Simon Peter bowed a farewell to the young men, he also turned and bowed to Moses, who nodded his head in approval.

He then looked over at Amnon and requested that he go up next.

The Storyteller Collection

Amnon's Story
Natural consequences for one's own actions

Let's face it: Amnon did not want to be here. But he knew that, when Jesus made a request, he had no choice. So, letting out a resounding sigh, he stood and walked nonchalantly toward the podium.

Now, Amnon was as handsome as his father had been in his youth; he had dark, thick curls, a strong brow, and a straight nose, but unlike his father, he had a weak chin. He was dressed in white robes with a gold-and-red shawl worn only by royalty. At the podium, he stood tall and straightened his shoulders to let these young men know that he was somebody.

"I am Amnon, first son of King David and Ahinoam. I was summoned by the Lord and Savior, Jesus, to submit to you my story.

"I was the eldest prince and heir to the throne of David. If you don't know who King David was, then you must have been living in a cave. For those who don't know my father, he was the one who slew Goliath in his youth. He was the only man who had God's own heart. I was brought up with privileges that none of my siblings had.

I emulated myself after my father—who else is one to emulate?

The Storyteller Collection

"My father had many wives and many concubines. I, too, had concubines, but I was still yet unmarried. By his actions, my father had shown me that I could have anything I wanted. As a child, I saw him take the woman Bathsheba and make her his own. It was rumored that my father had her husband, Uriah, killed at the front lines. If it happened, it was of no concern to me, as my father was the king. Bathsheba became one of my father's favorite wives.

"As always, people are interested in what occurred between me and my half sister, Tamar, so here it is. She was the daughter of my father and Maachah and the full sister of my half brother, Absalom.

"She was of no consequence to me until she came into her womanhood. She grew to be an extremely beautiful woman, with an innocence that seemed to tug at my heart. Each time I would see her, she would consume my thoughts and stir my loins in a way that no other had. Since I had never been in love, I was under the delusion that what I felt for her was love.

"As time went by, I seem to want her even more, but I knew the law, and, because of our customs, my father—the king—would never let me have her.

I tried to get her out of my head, but the more I tried, the more I wanted to lie with her. Wanting to be with her began to drive me to madness.

I began to feel weak and took to my bed, as I began to lose weight. Wasn't this, indeed, love? My cousin asked me one day what was wrong with me, so I confided in him. He told me what to do if I really wanted her. I asked, 'What about the king?' He told me not to worry. The king would be angry, but he would do nothing, for I was his firstborn son and the direct heir to his throne. On the other hand, Tamar was just his daughter— one of many daughters.

"So, on the advice of my cousin, I asked my father's permission for Tamar to cook me some food and serve it to me in my room. He agreed and summoned her to do so.

"The bottom line was that I took her, as I had desired her for far too long. She begged me not to, but I was not about to be denied after all this time. I don't know what exactly I expected, but I did expect far more than I got out of it. I found that it wasn't as good or as pleasurable as I had thought it would be. Disappointed, I had my servant throw her out.

"My cousin was right; the king was furious but did nothing, as I was his heir. I never saw Tamar again; I was told she that moved into the home of our brother, Absalom.

"Two years later, I was invited to a feast with the rest of my brothers by Absalom.

I thought it was a nice gesture to get all the sons of David together. How was I to know that Absalom held ill will against me because of his sister, Tamar? As I was drinking and enjoying myself, Absalom had his servants come upon me and slay me! Me—the heir to the throne! What was worse was that our father, the king, did not even avenge his firstborn son."

"Wow, that guy is heartless," whispered the second young man to his friend, "and he did his own sister!"

"Well, it takes one cold one to recognize another," countered his friend.

Absalom's Story
God said, "Vengeance is mine; I will repay!"
—Romans 12:19

Absalom had heard enough. He burned with anger as he listened to Amnon minimize his sister's worth once again. He felt that he had been misunderstood all this time, so he was glad to be here to set the record straight.

"You swine!" Absalom spat out, as he stood with a murderous glint in his eye.

"I should have killed you with my own hands instead of letting it happen at the hands of my servants." Though younger, Absalom was several inches taller than

Amnon, which made him a daunting figure as he advanced toward Amnon. Amnon seated himself quickly on the other side of Simon Peter.

Absalom caught a glimpse of Moses from the corner of his eye. He turned toward him slightly and saw him motion him to the podium. He tried to expel his anger from his chest as he turned toward the podium, replacing Amnon. Absalom, like all of David's sons, was also handsome; however, Absalom had a strong, commanding presence, unlike his brother Amnon. Amnon had been spoiled and had an air of entitlement about him. He never fought to show his leadership; he had just waited to inherit everything at no cost to him.

Absalom was different. He believed in earning his way. He did not sit around in royal robes; he was dressed in the fighting attire of trousers, a loose shirt, and a turban. His beard was full, his eyes were clear, and he had a commanding presence.

"Greetings, in the name of Jesus Christ, the Lord of good king David. I am David's third son, Absalom, born of Maachah.

"You see me here today as a warrior and a rebel. I met my end almost as a commoner, but I am getting ahead of myself. I wasn't always like this.

My mother, Maachah, bore my sister Tamar and me with King David. I was considered one of my father's favorite sons, and I was a favorite with our people as well. In my youth,

I was considered charming in manners; I was handsome and was proud to be part of the royal family. I adhered to all royal laws and made my father's God my God, as it was handed down. By obeying the laws of God and the king, I captivated the hearts of our people.

"Just like Amnon, I was a prince and lived in great style. I rode in a magnificent chariot with fifty men running before me. However, one dark day, my wife found my sister at our doorstep; she was dirty, her clothes were torn, and she was in great distress. She told the story of her rape and how our brother Amnon threw her out of his quarters like a beggar after he had taken all that she had.

"I am aware that customs have changed in this new time, but in our time, a young man would not marry a woman if she had been defiled in any way, whether it was by her design or not. Women only had their virtue and their ability to bear their husbands' children. When this was taken away from her, she had nothing else to show her worth. This was my little sister; she was a princess. She was royalty, and he had defiled her and faced no retribution.

"I burned with anger over what Amnon had done. I burned even more once I found out that my father was not going to do nothing about this tragic act performed on his daughter.

I couldn't help wondering why my father would send his daughter Tamar into the bedchamber of her half brother with no one to chaperone her. She was not his wife, nor was she a chambermaid. She was royalty. I personally felt that my father was as much to blame as Amnon.

"When my father did wrong, his God corrected him, yet he felt that he should not correct his heir to the throne? I felt that Amnon was not fit for the throne, and I swore to myself that he would never sit on it.

"I said nothing to my father, and I spoke nothing of this to Amnon. I never spoke of him, either good or bad. I just brought my sister to live in my household and took care of her.

"I bade my time for two years. I continued to go on with my business. I know I looked the same on the outside, but I had changed on the inside.

I burned with anger so much so that all I could focus on was avenging my sister. I had decided in those two years to set a trap for my brother and kill him. I had completed having my sheep sheared and decided to have a feast at the completion for all my brothers. I asked my father, the king, to allow my brothers to go.

I invited him as well, but I was well aware that he would not go. After I pressed him a bit, he agreed that all of my brothers could go to the feast.

"As the feast took place, Amnon was full of drink, that's when I had my servants strike him dead. Retribution is what I wanted at that time, but it was short-lived. Unlike Amnon, I feared our father's retaliation, so I fled. I stayed away for three years and finally reunited with my father. In the years that I was gone, I had changed. There was a bitterness that had aligned itself in my heart for my father. I was not held accountable for my actions against Amnon, as his actions against our sister were not held him for I, too, was a prince.

"I felt that my father was a weak king and that he was definitely not true father material. I began to think I would make a better king. In my anger, I lost sight of the fact that my father was anointed by God to be king...and I was not. To make a longer story short, I was killed by one of my father's men when I got tangled in a tree.

"Anger consumed me and made me lose sight of everything, including what our Lord and Savior had declared—that vengeance was His and that He would repay."

"Now, that dude is a guy after my own heart," exclaimed the second young man in a low voice to his friend. *"I would have done the same thing if that was my sister."*

The Storyteller Collection

"But guess what? That girl you had sex with was a virgin, too, and she is possibly somebody's sister," smirked his taller friend.

Jacob's Story
An Imperfect Man, Blessed by God

Moses nodded his thanks to Absalom as he took his seat. Jacob sat beside Moses, and he nodded to him that it was his turn. Jacob bowed with respect to him and rose, making his way to the podium. Jacob had been a strapping, good-looking man. Even in his youth, he had been quite clever.

He, too, had been an heir to a throne—the throne of Israel. Moses was anxious to hear how he told his story. Would it be about how he lied and cheated to get what he wanted? How he split the nation of Israel by playing favorites among his sons? Or would he tell that, though God revealed Himself to him, it had still taken Jacob a long time to become a true servant of the Lord. Jacob was now many years old. He had learned some harsh lessons during his life. He would hide nothing, as he made an account of his life's story.

"Greetings, in the name of our holy Savior, Jesus Christ." This was his preamble. "I am Jacob. You will have heard many times through the years that 'He was the God of Abraham, Isaac, and Jacob.'

"My forefather, what you would call 'grandfather' today, Abraham was a great man. He had followed God passionately and without reservations. He was blessed with my father very late in life, though he and my grandmother felt they would never have children. My father was obedient to his parents.

He never took on concubines in his youth. He married at forty years of age to my mother, whom my grandfather chose. My father was faithful to my mother, as he believed in following the doctrine of the Lord.

"Like my grandfather's story, it took years before my mother conceived my brother and me. But she did; she conceived twins. I have a twin brother. His name is Esau. We were fraternal twins; he was the first one born. We were so unalike. Esau was extremely red and hairy, and I was extremely smooth. Though my father took pride in both of us, he was quite fond of his eldest son, Esau. On the other hand, my mother doted on me.

"I don't know why, but I always wished I had been born first. I longed for my brother's birthright and even bartered with him for it once, when he was famished. Since we were born so late in our parents' lives, we were still young when my father's health began to fail due to his advanced age.

He felt that it was time to give his blessing before he died. Now, in our time, the father blessed his child who would supersede him in the family, who was usually the firstborn.

"I had not planned to obtain this all-important blessing, but, thankfully, my mother did. She had overheard my father ask my brother, Esau, to go and kill a wild boar and make him his favorite meal, for after he had eaten it, he would bestow upon him his blessing. My mother came up with a plan and told me she would fix the meal for my father. She told me to put on some of my brother's clothes and tie animal hair around my body. Why? Because my father's sight was just about gone, and he would not be able to see which son it was. This went off without a hitch, and I received my father's blessing.

"Needless to say, my brother was furious once he found out, and my parents thought it would be best for me to leave while my brother was in his rage. Otherwise, they would lose both their sons. So I was sent to my mother's brother's home. I didn't want to leave my homeland, but I didn't want to die, either, so I was resigned to go and stay with relatives until my brother's temper cooled.

"When I arrived at my uncle's, the first person I saw was this beautiful girl named Rachel. She was my uncle's daughter, and was she a sight to behold!

The Storyteller Collection

Within a short time, I requested of my uncle that he allow us to marry. I told him I would work for him for seven years just to make this remarkable woman my wife.

"My uncle agreed! Those years flew by for me. The more I got to know her over this time, the more I loved her. The day my seven-year agreement concluded, I was dizzy with anticipation. As I drank wine, I said to my uncle, 'Give me my bride, as my seven-year agreement has concluded.' He agreed, and plied me with more wine, as he prepared my wedding for me. I was so happy; I was almost giddy, as I was in a world all my own. I thought I married my beloved Rachel and consummated our union immediately.

"The day after my marriage, I found out that I had not married Rachel, but I had married Leah, her older and very plain sister! I had been tricked! I thought of Esau for a split second, wondering if this is what I deserved for the way I cheated him out of his birthright. I confronted my uncle about what he did. He said the eldest daughter must marry before the youngest one.

He then struck a new bargain; after the marriage week was over, he would allow me to marry Rachel as well, but I must work an additional seven years for her. I was so in love with Rachel that I would have worked twenty more years for her, but my uncle would never know this.

"As the additional seven years of servitude was being paid to my uncle, I became the father of ten sons. Then, finally my beloved Rachel gave birth to Joseph." As Jacob spoke Joseph's name at the podium, he glanced back at his beloved son, who had been sitting next to him on the stage.

Jacob continued. "It was around this time that I started having dreams. I remembered one dream in which God told me to pack up and leave my uncle's house. Joseph was young when I packed up all that was mine and headed back to my father's land. I was older then and a bit wiser.

Along the way, as I approached Canaan I sent messengers to my brother with gifts for him. I made amends to my brother by humbling myself before him and admitting that he was my lord. But my brother was happy with his lot in life and did not seek retribution.

"Some nights later, as I was alone in communion with God, an angel appeared, and I found myself wrestling with him. We wrestled all night. At daybreak, he touched my thigh, and, from that day on, I have had a limp. When I came to realize that this was a divine entity, I demanded to be blessed. He then said that my name was now Israel, which means 'the man who wrestled with God.'

"I felt like a nomad during this time. As I was traveling near Bethlehem, my beloved Rachel passed while giving birth to our youngest son, Benjamin. This was a hard time for me.

"I finally put down roots in Hebron. My family flourished here. It felt good to lay down roots again. My son Joseph was growing by leaps and bounds and he was truly a joy to my soul.

In him, I could see his mother, and my heart would swell with joy and thankfulness for the two sons she bore me.

"Sometimes, in a quiet place, I will admit that, if my uncle would have allowed me to have Rachel initially as promised, I would only have her two sons. I had no desire for anyone but her.

It's not that I don't love my other children; I just didn't love their mothers. I would always do right by my other sons and honor their birthrights, but I have to admit that Joseph, Rachel's firstborn, was the son I loved the most.

"I never dreamed that the love I had for my son Joseph would stir such hatred for him from his brothers, nor that they would sell their own flesh and blood into slavery. They told me that he had been attacked by a wild animal and killed.

"It is hard for me to relive the pain of losing my son Joseph at the tender age of seventeen, but I will turn this portion of my story over to Joseph. Through the years, God was always described as 'the God of Abraham, Isaac, and Jacob.'

How I wished they had added the name of my son Joseph along with ours!"

Joseph's Story
The Dreamer

Joseph stood and helped his father, clearly a broken man, back to his seat. Looking toward Moses, who gave him a nod to start his own story, he approached the podium. A smile creased his father's weathered lips, as he had just noticed that Joseph was wearing the coat of many colors he had made for him in his youth.

"Greetings, from our Lord and Savior, Jesus Christ," he started out. Joseph stood straight and tall with regaled dignity, as he had been only second to Pharaoh in his appointment. He still showed remnants of his look that mirrored Pharaoh's during those times, but he never forgot his heritage.

"As with all of us, I was blessed with a gift: the gift of dreams. I thought nothing of them as a child, to my detriment. I remember that, when I was seventeen, right after my father had given me the coat I am wearing, I had two dreams. The dreams were so incredible that I told them to my brothers. I did not know it was those two dreams that made my brothers plot my death.

The Storyteller Collection

"In my first dream, my brothers and I were gathering bundles of grain. Suddenly, the bundles of grain that had been prepared by my brothers gathered around me and bowed to me. In the second dream, there was the sun (father) and the moon (mother) and eleven stars (brothers) bowing down to me.

"Telling my brothers of my dreams infuriated them. They called me a dreamer. My father would send me out to check up on my brothers and report back to him. So while they were in Dothan, feeding the flocks, my brothers saw me coming toward them. They had already plotted to kill me, unbeknownst to me.

It was my eldest brother Ruben, who didn't want me dead. He suggested they throw me in a hole until they figured out what to do with me. I didn't know that Ruben had intended to rescue me and return me to my father at the time.

My brothers tackled me, stripped me of my beautiful coat of many colors that my father had made for me, and threw me in a hole. I heard my brothers talking among themselves of what to do with me, when I heard my brother Judah suggest killing me! I didn't believe this, but my brothers (at least most of them) wanted me dead.

"After a while, they pulled me up, and I thought they were through with this wickedness, but right then and there, they sold me to some perfume peddlers on their way to Egypt. My brothers received twenty pieces of silver for me.

"I couldn't describe how I felt, as I was carded off like a common slave. It was true that I fought with my brothers, but I never thought for one instant that they did not love me. I was seventeen when my brothers sold me into slavery, and I would never be free again.

"Once the caravan arrived in Egypt, I was sold to Potiphar, the captain of Pharaoh's guard. Being young, I learned things quickly, and before long, I was running Potiphar's household for him. By God's grace, everything to which I put my hand prospered. Potiphar's wife became attracted to me and wished that I would lie with her, but I refused, as I would not sin again God. At one point, I had to run from her aggressiveness, and she was so angry that she accused me of trying to rape her, which ultimately landed me in prison.

"Over time, as God was with me, the warden put me over the other prisoners. Not long after that, two of Pharaoh's servants were imprisoned for having offended Pharaoh. One was a cupbearer, and the other was the chief baker. Later, I remember that both had dreams the same night, so I offered to interpret them. In doing so, I interpreted that one would be put to death, while the other would obtain his station in life again. Within three days, the baker was hanged, and the cupbearer was set free.

The Storyteller Collection

I had beseeched the cupbearer to remember me to Pharaoh to help obtain my freedom. The cupbearer agreed, but once he was released, he forgot all about me. I languished in prison for another two years.

"About that time, Pharaoh had two dreams that disturbed him. His first dream was of seven lean cows, rising out of the river and devouring seven fat cows. His second dream was of seven weathered ears of grain devouring seven fat ears of grain. When no one could interpret his dreams for him, this is when the cupbearer remembered me interpreting his dream. I was called before Pharaoh and asked to interpret his dreams. I told him that he would have seven years of abundance followed by seven years of the worst famine that would ever hit his land. I advised Pharaoh to store grain during the years of plenty to offset the famine years.

"I was then blessed by being released from prison and put in charge of all the land of Egypt. Pharaoh gave me his signet ring and clothed me in fine linen and necklaces made of gold. I was renamed and given an Egyptian wife. At the age of thirty, I was the most powerful man in Egypt, next to Pharaoh. During the seven years of abundance, I worked hard, filling all the storehouses to capacity. During the years of famine, it was so severe that people from all over came to Egypt to buy bread.

"At this age, I had long since put my old life and family out of my mind. I was no longer a child, and, though I had power, I was still a slave. I still prayed to my father's God and still maintained my father's beliefs out of respect for him, but my life was not directed by me.

"It was during the second year of the famine that my father sent my brothers to Egypt to buy goods. I can still remember the day that I looked up and saw them. However, they did not recognize me, as I was no longer a boy but a man. I also looked like a true Egyptian at that time. My anger welled up in me after all of the years I had been in captivity. They had been allowed to stay within the family, but I had not been. Initially, I spoke only to them in the Egyptian language, using an interpreter to translate. I accused them of being spies; however, they pleaded with me that their only objective was to buy grain for their family, which included my little brother Benjamin. I demanded that their youngest brother be brought to Egypt.

"When they finally returned, they were afraid, but I gave them my best hospitality, as I was glad to receive not just my youngest brother but all my brothers. The next day, I secretly had a silver cup put in Benjamin's bag and had my servants search for it. When it was found, Judah pleaded that he be imprisoned and that his younger brother be allowed to return to their father.

I couldn't keep up this farce any longer. I sent my servants out of the room and finally revealed to them who I was.

"As you can imagine, they didn't believe this until I relayed the events of the last day they saw me. It was at that time that I saw fear in their eyes. I told them not to be concerned. What they had meant for evil, God had turned into good. I then told them to go and bring our father and their entire households into Egypt, as there were still five more years of famine ahead.

"Before I sit down, I just want you to know it had been more than twenty years since I had last laid eyes on my father. You have no idea what that was like. My father embraced me and cried; I cried, too. I have never let go of him from that day to this. Blessed be the name of the Lord for allowing me to depart from my family in order to help save their lives many years later."

Jacob rose as Joseph returned to his seat. They embraced again and seated themselves side by side.

Now, there were only two of them left to tell their stories: Moses and Paul. Moses realized that it is now his turn at the podium. He had never been good at dialogue; his brother Aaron had always been his mouthpiece. But things were quite different now as he walked up to the podium; God had given him a voice to praise Him from the hilltops, and Moses had since he left this earth.

Moses' Story
The Law Giver

Grasping the edges of the podium, he bowed his head and smiled. "Greetings. I come in the name of our Lord and Savior, Jesus Christ." His voice was clear and concise with no stuttering or trembling. His voice was deep, and he took command of the stage. Why hadn't he trusted in the Lord all those years ago, back when He was trying to let him know that He had his back? Well, at least Moses knew now.

"I'm sure you have heard my name once or twice in your life. I was given the distinct opportunity to lead the Israelites out of Egypt and into the land of milk and honey, as was promised to their ancestors Abraham, Isaac, and Jacob. I was also chosen to give the law, the Ten Commandments, to the people of Israel.

"I would like to introduce Joseph. It was he who brought the Israelites into Egypt for safety and protection at that time. I believe that Joseph had a far more telling dream prior to his departure of this life; he dreamed that his bones were to be taken when the Israelites left Egypt. He knew that it would come to pass, and he did not want his bones left behind there.

The Storyteller Collection

"About four hundred years later, as promised by God, the Israelites flourished and became many. The new pharaoh of that day saw us as a liability and therefore enslaved us as a people. When he had heard of a Savior coming, he did the unthinkable and had many baby boys slaughtered. Those were very tragic times.

"About that time, my mother gave birth to me. She hid me for three months, and, when she could hide me no longer, she put me in a waterproof basket and floated me up the Nile River. She didn't leave me alone; she had my older sister Miriam watch me as I floated up to the private quarters of the pharaoh's daughter. As I was told, she felt sorry for me. My sister came up to her and asked if she would like her to get a wet nurse to nurse him. She said yes, and, lo and behold, I was now being taken care of by my real mother, under the protection of the pharaoh's daughter! Talk about divine intervention.

"When I was a toddler, I was sent to live with the princess, and there I lived until I was about forty years of age. It was about this time that I found out about my lineage. I went down to the quarry where the Israelites worked, and I noticed a guard beating my fellow kinsman. I looked around to make sure no one saw and struck the guard dead. I thought this was a good thing; however, the next day, I saw that same kinsman arguing with a fellow kinsman and tried to get them to stop.

The first kinsman from the day before questioned me, asking if I were going to kill him like I had the guard. I then realized that he did not think it was a benevolent blow for justice but that I was simply a murderer.

"I realized I had to run for my life. I had heard that Pharaoh wanted me dead for this impetuous act of mine, and, to be honest with you, I was afraid. So I left all that I knew and traveled to an unfamiliar place to save my life.

"I found myself in the land of Midian and came upon a lovely maid drawing water from a local well. I assisted her, and, in return, she introduced me to her father. Well, as nature will take its course, I married her and dwelled in her land with her people. Let's see. I left Egypt when I was about forty years old and dwelled in this new land of Midian for about forty years. In this time, eighty years old was close to the end of one's life; however, back in my time, you were just hitting middle age.

"Let me not digress. I was content living there, tending to my father-in-law's livestock, enjoying my family. As I was tending the herd on the back side of a mountain, I noticed a flickering light; it was a bush that was on fire! It was strange, as it was on fire but had not been consumed.

"I suddenly heard a voice from the Lord letting me know that this was deemed a holy place and that I should treat it as such. The Lord conversed with me about what was happening to His people in Egypt. He had chosen me to get them out. I thought that God had made a mistake—me? I had not been in Egypt in forty years! I was not the best orator. As a matter of fact, I was old and slow, and I had a stutter at that time.

"The Lord said that He would handle all of that, but I was insistent that He find a real orator, not the likes of me. I argued with God. I asked, 'Who should I say is sending me? What if they don't believe me? What if, what if?'

"I will tell you the truth; I didn't want to do this. I knew that I was still wanted for murder in Egypt. I had a family now, and I didn't want to rock the boat. But God chooses whom He wants to do things, and He chose me. He offered my brother Aaron to speak on my behalf, and He sent me to free His people.

"I made a plea for Pharaoh to let the children of Israel go, but he would not. God sent ten plagues upon the land to show that He was not playing, and when the last one was visited upon the land, Pharaoh couldn't get rid of us fast enough. He actually paid us to go! We gathered all that was important to us and left that godforsaken place. Adding it all up, the Israelites had been in bondage for 430 years! We traveled by way of the Red Sea, thinking that this episode in our lives was over; however, it was not.

Pharaoh realized that he had lost a great commodity by letting us go. Who would be his slaves now?

"He ordered many chariots and the multitude of his armed forces to follow after us. Once we realized that Pharaoh was after us, the people began to complain about being slaughtered here in the wilderness. I called upon the Lord, and He told me to outstretch my hands over the sea—and it parted! The wind parted it, and we were able to walk through, completely dry. As the last of us came through, Pharaoh had begun to walk through as well. God told me to outstretch my arms once more, and the waters from each side came back together again, killing the Egyptians. None of them survived that fateful day.

"I would like to say that everything was good after that, but it wasn't. I fear that the Israelites had been in captivity for so long that they weren't used to freedom. They first complained of food, so the Lord gave them manna daily. They were told not to hoard it, as He would supply their food needs. However, they had a slave mentality and began to hoard it; they found the next day that it was inedible. They wanted meat, so they were given quail, yet they were never satisfied.

"They quarreled among themselves, so this was the time a judging system was created to hear grievances.

With two million people there at the time, you can imagine that there was a great need for laws to be implemented, so the Lord summoned me to give me His laws (commandments). I was only gone for forty days; however, when I returned, they had molded idols for themselves. This angered our Lord, and He thought of destroying them. I have to say that it angered me as well. But the Lord remembered the covenant He had made with their ancestors Abraham, Isaac, and Jacob, so in the end, the Lord did not destroy the Israelites. He did let them wander in the wilderness for forty years until that generation died off. That generation never saw the land promised by the Lord.

"Even to this day, it saddens me, because the Israelites saw firsthand what the Lord did to obtain their release from bondage. They saw that they never had a hungry day and that He protected them, all the while reminding them that they had an inheritance from Him simply because of who their ancestors were. He blessed them with the law—a guide, if you will—on how to govern their lives so that their years on this earth would not only be fruitful but immeasurably long.

He promised to give them a land known for its milk and honey. But above all this, He promised to always be with them and to go before them to ensure their safety...but that was simply not enough for them.

"I was 120 years old when I was called home. I am humbled by the fact that, as of today, I am the only human being who has ever spoken to the Lord face-to-face."

Moses bowed humbly as he went to seat himself. He glanced Paul's way, letting him know that he was the final of the seven to be heard.

Paul's Story
A Changed Man

"Greetings, in the name of our Lord and Savior," Paul greeted the audience.

"I am an apostle. I beg you not to confuse me with one of the original twelve disciples, as they were handpicked by Jesus and later became apostles after His death. I was converted into His service.

"I grew up with firm convictions and a fiery temper. I was against sacrilege in my day, and I believed that Judaism (which was actually Christianity) was a plague against God.

"In order for the Lord to put us on the courses He has chosen for our lives, He changes things about people that are not in alignment with His visions of them. I was born Saul of Tarsus, and I was such a person.

"I will be truthful; in my beginning as a young man, I was a tyrant.

I didn't understand what these people were professing about this new religion. We believed at the time in the teachings of Moses, so when the likes of Stephen tried to intertwine the teachings God handed down to Moses with this 'Jesus,' we all felt it that was sacrilegious. Yes, I was there the day Stephen was stoned to death. I did not participate, but I held the coats of the ones who did.

"I believed in ridding ourselves from these people who would try to alter the law. I brought many to justice based on what I believed at the time. I struck out in my truth and my beliefs. People came to know the name of Saul of Tarsus, and they feared me. I have to say that I took some delight in that honor. In my time, you would think me akin to the 'Hitler' of your day.

"One day, I came up with the idea that, if I got one of our high priests to give me a series of letters, I could take my tyranny on the road and flush out these heathens and bring them to justice in Jerusalem. Once this was approved, I headed to Damascus with some other comrades.
"My heart was hard against the Christians. Even the mere thought of them enraged me.

I did hateful things to them in the name of God. Because of my belief system then, I felt I was doing a good deed. That's what I was thinking as I pressed on to Damascus.

"But, brethren, let me share with you that your whole outlook on life as you know it can be changed in an instant by the Lord, Jesus Christ—as did mine. On that road to Damascus, I felt a sharp pain in my head, and I fell from my horse. I was on the ground, groaning with a pain I had never known. I was holding my head and trying to focus, but my sight had left me, and I found myself blind. That's when words were spoken to me. Jesus asked me one simple question: why was I persecuting Him?

"I knew this was the Lord, but which one? God? I was not persecuting God; I was doing all this in His name. I asked this sovereign Lord who He was.

"'I am Jesus, whom you are persecuting,' He replied. He then told me to get up and go into the city of Damascus. I hadn't gone insane, as the people I was traveling with had heard the voice also. They helped me up on my horse and led me into the city. I was completely blind for three days. During this conversion, I neither ate nor drank. Later, I realized that Jesus had to take away my sight for a time so that I could truly see. He emptied my stomach so that He could fill me with His anointment and righteousness.

"If anyone asked what the turning point in my life was, I feel that it was on the road to Damascus. I truly found my way there. During my sightless days,

I just prayed day and night, almost without ceasing. Jesus told me that I would regain my sight once Ananias came and baptized me, washing my sins away.

"Once I regained my sight, I knew my mission in life: to preach that Jesus was the Son of God. Now, this was not easy in the beginning. The people knew my name and my reputation. They knew that I had come there to take them as prisoners to the chief priests.

"Brethren, I am here to share with you that when you sully your name and reputation, it is an uphill battle to you to obtain your honor back. This, at the time, was my challenge. Since I had worked so fervently for evil, I was determined that, no matter what anyone said, I would work even harder for Jesus.

"I no longer relied on my reasoning and thoughts like a man; I simply made up my mind to serve Jesus Christ. My whole belief system had been changed. I had been resurrected from a dead life; I was called upon to be a deliverer of Jesus' good news.

"Before, I had thought there was only one God, of whom Moses spoke. I now know Jesus is the Messiah, who was promised by God beforehand, through His prophets in the Holy Scriptures.

"I believe that Jesus was born and died for our sins. I know that the law revealed the extent that sin had over people lives, and only Jesus' power can break its hold. I used to think that all who were not Jews were outside the covenant that God made with Israel. Now, I believe that gentiles and Jews are united as the people of God in Jesus Christ.

"Finally, I had believed that the violent persecution of the church was an indication of my zealousness for what I believed to be true. I now believed that hostility toward any of God's people was sinful, and one would incur the wrath of God. I thank my Lord and Savior for stopping me when my rage was at its highest.
"By Jesus' grace, He changed me. He changed my name, He changed my thoughts and ideals, and, in doing so, He changed me."

* * *

After Paul had concluded his story, he went back to his place, and all seven rose, bowed respectfully, and left the stage. Not one stayed to answer questions or mingle with the young men, for that was not their purpose. They had been sent to share parts of their life stories, as Jesus had commissioned them. Their stories were there to show that, from their time to this one, all had struggled with their manhood. They all had come to their "forks in the road" and had to decide this day, who to choose.

These young men were no different. They must make this choice on their own, as did these seven.

Epilogue

The men began to leave noisily, as the second young men was making his way toward his professor.

"Professor," he said, dodging the men who were trying to file out of the auditorium, "Where did they go?

I wanted to speak with a couple of them. Do you have their contact information? I have some questions."

"They weren't invited for a question-and-answer period," explained the professor. "They came a long way and had to get back. If you have questions, you can find their complete stories in the Bible."

"The Bible?" repeated the second young man. "Are you telling me that the stories they told are in the Bible? I thought the Bible was about God and Jesus. I thought it was about old stories of redemption and forgiveness. These guys sound like us, with real-life stories. Are you telling me that before Moses was the law giver, he murdered someone? A prince raped his own sister, and his brother had him murdered? Paul was akin to Hitler in his ruthlessness?

And Simon Peter betrayed Jesus by denying Him and held his guilt in his heart up until the day he died? Are you telling me that this stuff is in the Bible?"

"Yes," the professor stated truthfully. "Do you think what is happening now is 'new'? The things that are happening now have been happening since the beginning of time. King David was not only a great king and a man after God's own heart but he was also self-centered and self-absorbed, and he was a bad father.

"Jacob was the father of the twelve tribes of Israel, as was promised by God, but he also was a thief. He stole his brother's birthright and was a liar; he pretended that his wife was his sister in the hopes of saving his own skin.

"Judah, head of one of the twelve tribes of Israel, helped sell his brother Joseph into slavery, although his first thought was to kill him.

"Did you think that only the pharaohs, guards, and money lenders of that day were bad or evil? The Bible states, 'All have sinned and come short of the glory of God.'

Jesus did not sugarcoat their lives because He called them out to be great men. He wanted all to know that, even with flaws; He loved them and wanted to make them better men.

The Storyteller Collection

"I prayed to Jesus for help here, as I wasn't reaching any of you young men. He answered my prayers by simply sending seven men from the pages of time to share their stories and tell how their decisions shaped their lives—some for better and some for worse.

"Jesus will lead and guide you, love and protect you, and save you from all of your sins. What He won't do is take away your power to choose Him or man."

End

The Storyteller Collection

Marie Browders'
The Storyteller©

The Winding Road

The Storyteller Collection

The Storyteller Collection

The Winding Road

For the good man is not at home, he is gone on a long journey.
Proverbs 7:19

This is dedicated to men who want to rethink their life's stories and begin again.

The path was long and inevitable. Many had walked this same path to their final destinies, and this man was no exception.

As he walked the winding road, his hands began to sweat, as he clutched his life's file in his right hand tightly. He walked unhurriedly down this winding road, wondering if Jesus would understand how he had chosen to live his life.

He unconsciously began to move his file from one hand to the other; it somehow felt heavier now than before. He suddenly had a desire to see what was written in his file. He knew that, if he could just read it beforehand, he could give Jesus a better explanation of the decisions he had made in his life.

Beads of sweat rose on his forehead as he continued to walk.

The Storyteller Collection

He glanced down at his folder; it was a nondescript, long, beige folder with a seal of closure on it. Even though it had not been told to him, he knew this file was for Jesus' eyes only.

He began to walk slower, looking around at others on the winding road. Some had their heads up high and walked with conviction. Some had broad smiles as they ran down the winding road to its end. There was also some who tried to turn back but were halted by seven archangels: Michael, Gabriel, Raphael, Uriel, Simile, Oriphiel, and Zacharias.

So, there he was, a man on his final journey, on his one last walk. As the man walked, he mentally began to search through his life. He didn't have to read the file; he could remember his whole life almost verbatim.

He thought of his childhood; it was pretty average. He had a mother and a father in his home while growing up. He was not physically or emotionally abused. On the contrary, his parents were Christians and had taught him and his two sisters according to God's Word.

His parents had raised his siblings and him up in the church. They spoke constantly of how much God loved them. He was taught at an early age to ask God to forgive him if he had sinned, and he did that as a child.

He felt a bit better now. Jesus would see that he had been brought up in the right way by two loving parents. And he hadn't been a rebellious child, either. He had honored his mother and father. Thinking back to his childhood, he let out a sigh of relief and began to walk a bit faster. Yes, Jesus would see that he was not a bum on the street without upbringing. This man knew of Jesus.

His mind went to his high school years. His academics had earned him a four-year scholarship to the university. He remembered how proud his parents had been, as they did not have the funds to send him on to college for higher learning. He had been proud, too; he could finally get out from under his parents' thumbs and begin to live his own life.

"Wow," he thought, "where did that thought come from?" He was thankful for his parents, wasn't he?

He remembered his last summer as a teen; he had wanted to hang out with his friends and do whatever he wanted. However, his parents would not allow it. They chose to send him to a Christian summer camp. They felt that a Christian camp would give him direction and keep him focused on what really mattered in life, before his time in college.

He had been very angry about that. It didn't matter that once he had arrived and had begun to participate, he had had great fun. That was not the point. He was seventeen and almost an adult; they should have let him plan his own summer. Once he graduated from high school, he was happy that he was leaving home. He picked a university as far away from his parents as possible so that they would not try to rule his life ever again.

When he was far away at a notable university, he was thrilled to finally be on his own. He had the power to choose his own life's path then. He could come and go as he chose. He could choose his own friends, his own food, his own style of clothing—every decision was his to make.

When Sundays rolled around, one of the last things on his mind was church. He felt that he had had enough of going to church to last him a lifetime. When the Christian students tried to get him to participate in their activities, he would just ignore them.

He was an intelligent man and an apt pupil. College was perfect for him, as it steered him toward his life's goal. He had decided to become a doctor.

"You see," he thought to himself, "I became a doctor. I helped people. Jesus could not help but admire the kind of man I was in life."

As the man's mind lingered over his early college experiences, he suddenly began to think of other things he did at college. He had dabbled in drugs, but he thought that almost everyone did. When he and his peers had to pull all-night study sessions, he felt that he needed something to keep him up. He thought he was in total control during those times.

While in college, he had gotten a girl pregnant and had coerced her to have an abortion. He felt justified in doing this by the fact that neither one of them was ready for parenthood. He promised to marry the girl once they graduated. The girl, believing him, complied.

The moment she had the abortion, he dumped her. As these thoughts entered into his head, his pace slowed again. He had forgotten about that.
However, in his eyes, she had been trying to control his life, just like his parents had before her, and he had no desire to have that happen.

He felt that if he continued with her, she may have gotten pregnant again, and with the way she was acting, he couldn't possibly talk her into another abortion. At this point in time, he had to be a bit more careful. So did he choose abstinence at this time? Of course not; condoms became his ally against premature fatherhood.

The Storyteller Collection

As the man walked, he began to think of those long four years in college. In his second year, with the drugs, girls, and all-night parties, he found himself doing not very well. He was concerned that he may lose his scholarship and have to move back home. Some of his friends had told him about this "plain" girl who was consistently on the dean's list. He went out of his way to meet her. With a little flattery and a few idle promises on his part, they began to date. Over a short period of time, he had convinced her to write most of his papers, which kept his grades up. By the time he had reached his fourth year there, he had become more focused on his studies, and he dumped her. He then graduated with honors.

Now, the man had a modest four-year degree, but that would not get him to the position he wanted as a doctor. He applied to, and was accepted into, medical school. But medical school was not cheap, and apart from his college loans, now he had to take on a job just to make ends meet. In medical school, he was truly struggling.

He would do small, unethical things to get by, like borrowing a stethoscope from an intern nursing student and never returning it or paying someone else to write his papers. But these things, he felt, were harmless little issues.

It was not like he was stealing; he was going to be a doctor, and he needed to be a bit more creative to succeed.

The man rolled these things over his mind as he walked the winding road. Suddenly, the word "stealing" entered his head.

He remembered how his mother would say to him as a child, when he would take something that did not belong to him, "Son, it doesn't matter how small it is; it is still stealing. You have to make amends and ask God to forgive you."

All these years, he had always called it "borrowing," when, in actuality, he had stolen some of the equipment he needed from the kindness of others for his own selfish reasons. He had paid for work he did not do because he felt he could. He had not only been a thief but a liar as well.

In his second year of medical school, things became even harder for him. One day, some of his peers were talking about how they dated newly graduated nurses in an effort to get them to help pay for their education. They said that they didn't care if the women were ugly and fat; these girls were ready, willing, and able to help, with the hopes of landing a doctor as a husband.

"Oh, no," he moaned, as his mind settled on the actions of his youth.

Four weeks later, he met a woman he felt was truly beneath him. But he dated her and implied that he was interested in marriage once he completed his residency. She believed that his feelings for her were genuine and decided to help him in every way she could. She allowed him to move into her apartment in an effort to save rental fees and the like. She paid for everything, so he did not have to pay for even a morsel of his food.

This truly eased up his financial obligations. Over time, he began to ask her for help with his tuition fees, and she obliged. With this, he was able to quit his job and focus totally on his studies.
He became a doctor of internal medicine with honors. As was his plan all along, in his last year of residency, he broke off his "engagement" with the nurse, stating that he felt they had too little in common to continue the relationship.

The man paused on the winding road; he had forgotten how he had obtained his degree in medicine. He had forgotten how this nurse had literally paid his way through, and he had never even given her a second thought over these past fifty-five years.

For the first time, he wondered what had happened to her. The realization of her destiny was revealed to him, and he found she had never married. His selfishness had altered her destiny and, ultimately, her life.

This was a woman who had given him so much and whom he never gave a second thought.

"But why should that be my fault?" he rationalized to himself. "Relationships end; that's a part of life. She should have gone on to her next relationship. She chose not to marry, not because of me." Deep down inside, though, the man knew what he had done was wrong. Once again, he had stolen.

This time, it was a person's love and affection, as well as the person's money. His grandfather, in his old-fashioned way, had told him when he was young, "If a man will lie, he will steal." He had never understood what that meant in all these years, and now he did. He had lied to her about his feelings for her to steal her valuables. He had stolen lodging, food, tuition, sex, and love from her.

But surely, Jesus would understand that was just the stupidity of his youth. If he had known it would do that much harm, he would not have done it. Why would Jesus blame this on just him? A lot of the guys were doing it; it had not just been him.

"But I became a doctor," he defended himself. "That should account for something. I had a career helping people. Sometimes, the ends justify the means, and at the end of the day,

I helped people."

He was right. As the years went by, he had become an accomplished physician. He earned a name for himself and was honored. He was one of the foremost medical internists in the state. But he had one character flaw: if it didn't benefit him in some way, he was not interested.

There was an elderly person who was in need of his expertise. He handed the person off to a colleague. There was nothing in it for him. Unbeknownst to him, the doctor he passed the elderly patient off to misdiagnose her, and, by the time it was corrected, the patient had died.

Now, he justified his position on the case. "How is that my fault? I simply did not accept the case. I did refer her to another doctor. I have a right to choose which cases I take on. And this patient was old and about to die anyway."

But the nagging feelings of guilt did not go away. It suddenly became clear to him that he *never* took on cases from the poor.

His rationale was that his education had been expensive, and he was not going to waste it on someone who couldn't afford him. That was what free clinics were for.

As the man put one shaky foot in front of the other, he felt that he didn't want to think of his life anymore. It had not been as bad as other people's lives.

He hadn't begged anyone for anything. He had never been a burden on God; he had made his own way through life. Jesus had to let that account for something!

All his life, he would hear people beg Jesus for help with anything from paying a light bill to buying them a house—sheesh! He had never done that. He had gone to school and worked hard and provided for himself and his family. That's right—his family! He was a good, honorable man.

Ten years after becoming a doctor, he had married. He and his wife had three children together. And after his father died, he provided for his mother until her death, too.

A slow, smug smile came spreading across his face, as he thought of those attributes. Jesus had to see all this good he had done.

The Storyteller Collection

However, once again, his earthly life's walk replayed in his head like a DVD recording as the nooks and crannies of his character unfolded. He had not been celibate during those single ten years. He had had his fair share of girlfriends and one-night stands. He had had women get into catfights over him because of his lies and deceit. Most of these women felt they were going to marry him, but he had no intention of getting married then.

He was a single, good-looking doctor who was unattached and planned on staying that way.

Women would throw themselves at him, too—so what if he took what was offered? He was only a man, and a man had needs. He would take this one particular woman with him to special functions and affairs because she was sophisticated, elegant, and well-educated. He would date this other woman when he wanted to do something raw and spontaneous, and she was very adventurous. And then there was his "friend with benefits." She, like him, did not want any strings attached, and that is why they saw each other long after he married.

In the end, he didn't marry any one of those women. He was bored with them. He married for position in the community; he literally married the boss's daughter.

You see, her father was the head of a big-name hospital and was on the board of several prestigious committees of which the man desired to be a part.

He knew he had nothing in common with his wife when he married her. He didn't love her; he needed her. And he felt that she was getting something out of it, too; she married an ambitious doctor who was determined to go places.
Under the circumstances, he felt it had been a successful marriage.

They were married for over twenty-five years. During that time, he had had a host of affairs, not to mention the long-standing one with his "friend with benefits," until she decided to get married herself.

He did not feel guilty in the least. He felt his wife knew that theirs was not a real marriage but a merger, and she got as good as she gave. After twenty-five years, her looks had faded. After she had three kids, he couldn't even stand to look at her disgusting, out-of-shape body anymore.

During the marriage, his father died, and he told everyone he was too busy to attend the funeral, but that was not true. His father had disapproved of how he treated his wife and children. He had disapproved of how he was never there for them. He and his father did not see eye to eye on a lot of things.

The Storyteller Collection

His father kept throwing it in his face, saying that he had been raised better than that. You'd think he beat his family, which was the furthest from the truth. His wife had never worked; he provided everything for his family. But it was true that he was rarely there. He had not been there for any of his children's births.

But it was her decision to have so many children, not his. One would have been sufficient for him. With so many children, she had little time for him, so he had to go where he could get some attention for himself.

He was relieved when his father died; he no longer had to hear the lectures about family and God and character—sheesh! His mother was old then and couldn't live on her own. His two sisters tried to get him to take her in because of size of his house, but he flatly refused. He was around hospital smells all day and had no desire to have those same smells in his own home. He offered to pay for a good rest home. He felt that she would get adequate care in a rest home. But his sisters wouldn't have it, and they took their mother in, so he paid the expenses.

Some time after that, his wife's father retired as the head of the hospital, and he became his successor. Pride filled him, as he felt he had waited long enough for this status. A year later, his wife's father died, and he filed for divorce a few days later.

The Storyteller Collection

He married his young assistant two days after the divorce was final. He was crazy about her. They had been having an affair for some time when he filed for a divorce from his wife. This was the woman of his dreams. She was beautiful, sexy, cultured, willing in bed—everything a man wanted.

The man and his new wife had one child together, and, with him being a bit older now, he spent lots of time with this second family.

He rarely spoke to his children from his first marriage; it was as though they no longer existed.

The man felt his life that was now complete. He had everything he had ever wanted. He had worked hard for his dream life. So what if he had to walk over a few people to get to it? This was a dog-eat-dog world, and he was in it to win it.

Now, the man was married to his second wife until her death four years before his. This event made him really feel his mortality. She had been the love of his life. He was now older and was lonely. The child he had had with her had died ten years before in a car accident, and now he had no one.

His solitary, retired existence made him try to reconnect with his children from his previous marriage, but his effort failed. They had families and lives of their own now.

Since he had had no desire to have them in his life back then, there could be no true relation now, other than their acknowledging him as their biological father.

He remembered how he had so wanted to reconnect with his two sisters to whom he hadn't spoken since their mother died many years ago, but one had preceded him in death.

The other had Alzheimer's and no longer knew who he was.

Over his last four years, he thought of his parents often and of their teachings when he had been a child. He had tried to reconnect with his faith. But in reality, he wasn't trying to reconnect with his faith as much as he was grieving his loss. As he sat in the pews of the church, he felt angry, because his life was no longer as it had been. He wanted to know why Jesus had taken his wife and his child from him.

He wasn't trying to ask Jesus' forgiveness over all he done wrong in his life. He still felt that he was entitled. He did not seek solace in Jesus' Word; he felt solace in his bitterness. His nieces and nephews tried to reach out to him, and he turned them away, because he felt they were trying to get to his vast wealth.

At the time of his death, the man was disconnected from everything and everyone.

He had died alone. In life, he never thought once of how he treated other people.

His parents for whom he held no respect…
The girl he coaxed into an abortion that he never thought of again…

The plain girl he dumped after she wrote all his papers…

The people from whom he stole who trusted him…

The nurse who supported him through medical school…

The women he had had for every occasion…
The poor and elderly whom he would not help…
The wife he married with an agenda…
The siblings he ignored…

The children from his previous marriage whom he ignored all their lives…

The second wife and child he treasured more than God…

He had never showed love and respect to anyone other than his second wife. He never felt any remorse over his actions, not even when he turned to Jesus for compassion and help. He felt such pain and trepidation at his life's end. Had he never thought of the lives he affected?

The Storyteller Collection

The women he had lied to get to where he wanted to go? He had always felt that they were inconsequential.

As he took his last walk toward his Lord and Savior, the true realization of his life washed over him like torrential rain. He really wanted to pray now.

He wanted to fall down on his knees and ask the Lord to forgive him; alas, it was too late.

There were no prayers on the winding road that would have been heard. The moment one passes from life to death, there is a period of reflection, and that is down the winding road. It was over, and he knew it.

If he had just taken the time to put himself in others' shoes, he would have been able to see things from a different side of life. When problems arose in college, he could have called on Jesus for assistance, but he felt his way was the best for him. With one prayer, he would have opened a world of possibilities to himself. He realized these things now, here on this winding road.

He no longer needed to guess what was in the folder he was carrying. He knew. He knew that there would not be anyone at the end of this road who would stand up for his character as a man.
The winding road had begun to narrow, and he found himself in a single-file line.

The Storyteller Collection

His heart was so heavy, and he tried desperately to figure out what he would say to Jesus.

How could he explain all that he had done—how he had chosen to live his life and how he had chosen to ignore Him his entire life? How could he justify himself?

It was quiet as the man approached the throne. Finally, he was there, second in line. The person in front of him faltered, as Jesus looked in the book of life. Not seeing his name, He had him ushered away. The man walked up and saw Jesus there on the throne. Jesus had such compassion in his face that the man could not bear it, and he just walked away.

End

The Storyteller Collection
I Remember
(The Man on the Throne)

Finally, I'm fourth in line.
I look back to see at what a crowd behind.
No one was talking; you couldn't even hear a groan,
Everyone was watching the man on the throne.

People stood straight with their files in hand,
Hoping there mistakes, he would surely understand.
Each one was asked of their life's explanation
And judged accordingly, without any hesitation.

Now each was asked to make a simple comment,
"Do you remember it I who gave you your talent?"

One ahead of me faltered,
the next just walked away.
The third began to lie and
He said, "Depart from me this day!"

...and now it was my turn and I had to face him alone,
this just and kind Man on the throne.
Now everything was quiet and every mouth was neigh,
As he asked me as those before what did I have to say?
...and I looked at Him and said...

I remember, when I was a child;
How much I loved you,
how much you made me smile.

I remember, our walks alone;
We'd talk awhile,
then You would see me home.

I remember your soft eyes...
...oh in them, I could see the skies.
And now you ask me, if I can,
Remember your love and on it take a stand?

I say yes!, Yes, I can.
For I remember the throne and
I remember the Man.
...and what I've said is all so true,
for Jesus, you see...I remember you.

© 1984 Marie Browders

The Storyteller Collection

Marie Browders'
The Storyteller©

Home

The Storyteller Collection

The Storyteller Collection

Home

To my beloved mother, welcome home!

A little, nondescript black woman knocked on the door of a real estate agency.

"Come in, come in." The agent waved the woman in. "Have a seat, please."

The agent was on the phone as she motioned the woman in. She concluded her conversation and hung up the phone, smiling at her new buyer.
"Good morning, ma'am." The agent smiled.
"Hello," the black woman said hesitantly. "I really don't know what I'm doing here..."

"Why, you're here to choose your new home."
"Oh, I've always wanted a home of my own, but I could never afford one."

"Well with all the special discounts, you can afford one now." The real estate agent smiled.
"Do you really think I could? I mean, really?"
"Yes, really. This is what I'm here for: to fit people into their new homes."

"I don't have great credit, and my income is suspect. I just don't want to waste your time." The woman was clearly worried that she would not qualify.

The Storyteller Collection

"You're not wasting my time. Now, let's get started. How many bedrooms are you looking for?" the real estate agent inquired, as she readied herself to input the information into her computer.

"Well, two bedrooms will be sufficient."

"Two bedrooms?" The real estate agent looked over her glasses at the woman. "This is heaven; it's your chance to get whatever you'd like. This will allow you to get everything you ever dreamed of in a home of your own, so don't shortchange yourself. Need I remind you that there are special programs to assist you? Plus, there is an amazing Benefactor doing great philanthropic work; He will step in with closing costs to ensure that you get exactly what you want. So tell me, what do you really want?"

"Are you sure? If this is true, then I've always wanted a four-bedroom, Mediterranean-style home. I want to make sure that I have plenty of room for my granddaughter to live with me again; I've dreamed of this forever."

"Now, that's more like it!" The agent smiled as she began to enter this information in her computer. "How many bathrooms would you like?"
"I would love to have three."

"That's wonderful. Now, do you want one of the bedrooms to be the master and one of the baths to be the attached to the master bedroom?"
"Could I...I mean, yes, I would love that!"

The real estate agent entered this information in her computer as well. "Okay, do you want hardwood floors?"

"Oh, yes. Brazilian hardwood floors, if I may."
"You may."

"Sculptured, tufted carpet in the bedrooms?"
"Oh, that would be lovely in the bedrooms."
"Okay, are you looking for a living room with a family room, or would you prefer one large great room?"

"I really would like a formal living room with a separate family room."
"Fireplace?"
"Fireplace?"

"Yes, do you want fireplaces in the living room and the family room, too?"

"Could I have one in each of the rooms?"
"Of course, you can! Do you want crown molding and chair rails?" asked the agent.
"I've always loved those."

"Okay. In your kitchen, would you like a butler's pantry?"

"I've always dreamed of a butler's pantry."
"Fine. Now, back to your kitchen—what about Tuscan style?"
"Oh, my. That would be the kitchen of my dreams. Can it have glass inlay in the cabinet doors and brushed nickel hardware?"
"Of course. What about a farm sink?"
"No. I'd rather have a stainless-steel sink, please."
"Then, stainless-steel double sinks it is. Stainless-steel appliances?"
"Yes, please," the woman said, almost giddy.
"Now, it was brought to my attention that you had a desire for a tin ceiling."
"Yes. It was always one of my dreams."
"Okay, so we'll add granite countertops, a glass backsplash, and custom tile floors. Now, I know that you'll require a laundry room; how about a front-loading washer and dryer, with Shaker cabinets to encircle the entire laundry room?"
"Exactly!"

"Okay. Finally, the backyard—landscaped. With or without a pool?"
"No pool, but I would love a veranda."
"Okay, a home this size will be approximately four thousand to six thousand square feet."

"Really? Oh, my."

"This, of course, will come fully furnished. It comes as a package deal."

"Furnished? How much will this cost me?"

"As I have said before, you don't have to concern yourself cost. It's all covered. Okay, I think I have all the information I need, so let me show you some homes that will meet your criteria."

***

"Okay, so this is the first Mediterranean home I'm showing you. As you can see, it's on a cul-de-sac, with a lovely lake in the back of the property. It is beautifully landscaped, with a three-car garage and, more importantly, no pool."

"Wow! I could never afford this!" The woman turned to walk away.

"Why do you feel you are not worthy of a home like this? Please, tell me your story."

"Well, I was born in the Deep South; in Texas. We were quite poor, so I accepted my lot in life. From the time I was a little girl, I dreamed of owning my own home. When I became of age, I married a religious man of God—or so I thought. We had five children: four girls and a boy. Over time, my husband began to change and appeared to have lost his faith.

"Since he had fathered so many children in our town outside our marriage, he decided to leave

and relocate to California for better opportunities. He told me that he would send for us once he had settled there. So we waited in Texas for him to send for us, but he never did. When he would call home, he would say to me to wait and that he would send for us soon. I believed him.

"You see, I was a small slip of a girl when I met him. At twelve, I had had a stroke. So whenever I would attempt to smile, my face would be crooked. The other children would laugh at me, so I trained myself not to smile; this would make me at least look normal.

"My self-esteem was quite low, so when I met this handsome, well-mannered mulatto man in the church, I was smitten. He took notice of me also, I believe, I intrigued him, as he had never seen me smile; therefore, he felt I was aloof, but I wasn't aloof at all. I was over the moon about his attention to me.

"In our small town, it was well known that he had had several affairs, but I felt if I were to divorce him, I would have no one. And our faith was against divorce. So, time after time, I forgave him.

"When he left town for better opportunities, I didn't really believe him, but I was his wife, and I would not disrespect him or my marriage.

Things got too hard for us in that sleepy little town, so without his knowledge or permission, after he was gone for three years, I decided to follow him to California. I had no knowledge that he was living with a woman or that she had borne him a son. When I showed up on his doorstep with our five children, he was shocked. When I saw his arrangement with this woman, I yelled and screamed at him, and he had me committed to a mental institution!"

"Are you serious?" The real estate agent was incredulous.

"Yes, I am. I didn't know what was happening with my children, so I prayed and prayed for God to deliver me from that place. Finally, after a few months, I was released from that god-awful place, and I found a place to stay with some Christian people. They helped me to locate a little place of my own, and I acquired my children back from my husband. I once again thought of divorcing him, but I didn't believe in divorce; however, I felt that I could no longer be his wife.

"He continued to live with woman after woman, and I lived on the other side of town, raising my children. Though I went to nursing school, I mostly kept children in my life.

"I would hear from him from time to time, when he was feeling low or guilty, but I would just speak civilly to him and keep living my life.

I lived in the church, because it was my sanctuary, and it kept me grounded and sane. I kept my children in church as well. I was determined that they would become the best that they could be.
"As time went on, my children didn't turn out as I had hoped they would; they became selfish and self-centered. I believed that this was my fault, as they saw how I allowed their father to treat me, so I continued to pray for them, hoping they would change.

"As time went on, I became old, but my desire for a home was still as great as ever. However, it was never to be."

"You've left out some things," the real estate agent reminded her. "How you embraced the less fortunate and raised a twelve-year-old who only wanted a mother in her life. You denied yourself in order to see to it that your children would succeed in life. You sent for all of your husband's children so that they could attend his funeral. You had planned to apply for your husband's social security when you found out that he still had two children under the age of eighteen, so you did not apply for his benefits until these children were eighteen and no longer eligible for his benefits.

The Storyteller Collection

You have been there for so many.

"Though you could not impact some of your children's lives, you did impact that little twelve-year-old, who grew up and became a notable author of Christian books, which would not have occurred if you had not influenced her life. Thereby, she influenced others.

"The Father sent a special note to me to ensure that your home—your first home—is everything you had ever desired to have, and he said price is no object."

"H-he said that?" This little black woman stuttered, with a tear creeping down her cheek.
"Yes, I have it here in my notes."

"Oh, my..." was all she could say.
"Now, can we continue our home search now?"
"Well, if He said this, then I guess its okay."
"Now, as I said, there is a lovely creek in the back of this property—oh, and it has a veranda in the back!"

"I am overwhelmed—this is simply unreal!"
They entered an immaculate home with warm, muted colors on the walls. Some rooms had wallpaper, and some didn't. There were Mediterranean influences all through this home; it was a true sight to behold.

"This is just the first house. We have more for you to see."

"You mean there are homes prettier than this one?"

"Well, all these homes are lovely; you just have to choose."

"Let's go to the next home."

They went on to the next home, which was a truly stately manor. This next one had tall ceilings, Mediterranean columns, and a front veranda. There was a casita on the side of the home, as well as a six-car garage.

Inside, there were travertine floors and columns. The kitchen held commercial-grade appliances and had a fantastic view of backyard. This home also had a Koi pond.

"This one includes everything on your list of desires," the real estate agent pointed out.

As they walked out of the home, the black woman said, "You are so kind and patient. You are a great agent."

"Thanks, but though I've always been a businesswoman, I was not always a real estate agent. You can find my story in Proverbs 13; I am known as the virtuous woman.

The Storyteller Collection

"I have always been industrious; my husband always said I was worth my weight in gold. My husband revered me and put his whole trust in me.

I was determined to always respect and do well by my husband all the days of my life. I used to work with wool and other textiles; I would sell to merchant ships.

"I always rose early and fed my whole household, including my servants. I was always mindful of the poor and needy. I would make beautiful textiles of silks and purples and offer them to many, poor and rich alike.

"Because of my industriousness, my husband was well-regarded at our gates and sat among the elders of our land. I used to make fine linens and sell them for profit, delivering them to the merchants of our day. I was clothed in honor and wise in mind. I spoke with wisdom and kindness.

"I always held my household in high regard and never ate the bread of idleness. My children would rise early, always blessing me, as I would bless them. My husband would honor me, saying that there were many daughters of virtue but I excelled them all!

"The Lord felt that, in this stage of my life, I would be a notable real estate agent, as I would bring to the table all the effort and zeal I did in my other business. I exalt the Lord for thinking me capable of this position."

"Wow!" exclaimed the black woman. "You're 'that' virtuous woman? You have been revered for all times."

"You can revere me, but understand that I am not greater or lesser than you. You have got to realize that you are one of God's greatest gifts, and you deserve everything He has sent me to offer you. You deserve not only a home but a spectacular home of your choosing. So can we continue our home tour now?"

The black woman smiled brightly, giving no notice to her crooked smile, and said, "Yes, let's!"

The real estate agent then showed her an enchanting Cliffside Mediterranean home with a view that seemed to go on forever. It had a huge entry door of wrought iron and glass. A beautiful, intricate tapestry hung on the wall. Solid-wood floors with walnut-inlayed stripping went completely around the parameter of the living room. There were moldings and hand-carved vaulted ceilings. This home simply took her breath away.

"From the look on your face, I think this is the one, eh?" said the real estate agent. She smiled, closing her folder.

"Oh, yes!" the black woman exclaimed, "This one is magnificent! It has everything I have ever dreamed of and more.

The Storyteller Collection

It has a lovely master bedroom for myself and a lovely room for my grand

daughter, Twyla. I couldn't dream of a lovelier home than this. I thank God for this amazing home!"

"Good! Then this is your new home. As you can see, it is fully furnished to your taste. It has every amenity you could ever want. The Father was hoping that you would like this one the best!"

"Well, what do I have to do to acquire it? I mean, what papers do I have to sign?"

"Oh, my child, everything is done."

"Done? Really? Do you mean it's mine, just like that?"

"Have you forgotten that, in the Father's house, there are many homes? If it were not true, He would not have said so. He went to prepare a place for you. He wanted to make sure that you would be happy with your chosen home. He worked on this home diligently to ensure that it was exactly suited to you and your specific needs. He so wanted to bless you with an exquisite home."

The real estate agent walked to the door to take her leave. She smiled at the lovely little black woman and said, "May God bless you. Welcome home."

End

The Storyteller Collection

Epilogue

My beloved mother-in-law's one and only dream was to own a home of her own. I remember that we would talk late into the night of this desire of hers.

She had given so much to so many. I promised her that, one day, I would obtain a home for her, even though I couldn't afford one for myself.

As time went by, I would then tell her that she would always have her own bedroom in my home. Each time I would move, she would say, "Where is my room?"

I would tell her of her room in my house, all bright and sunny—although when she spent the night at my home, she would sleep on the floor because of her bad back.

My mother-in-law was called home in October of 2003. The one thing that saddens me was the fact that I wasn't in a position to buy her that home of her own before the Lord called her home. One day, as I worked on my stories, it dawned on me that I could give her a home—in one of my stories. So, Mother, welcome to your new home.

The Storyteller Collection

King Solomon once said, "What has been will be again, what has been done will be done again; there is nothing new under the sun."

Ecclesiastes 1:9 (NIV)

Hello. My name is Marie Browders, and I am known as the Storyteller.

But I'm not your typical storyteller; I tell stories, for adults. I believe that adults need their own brand of 'fairy tales' to remind them of what's important in life.
To remember that certain crossroads along the way need to be re-explored from time to time. Things like revisiting the character of man in the "Winding Path". Not giving up in the darkest of times with "The Relative". One of the stories that will make you re-think your integrity is "Telling Lies". These and other stories in my series of "The Storyteller" are to be stepping stones back to what God's plan for us was really meant to be.

"You see, I want you to be the very best you can be;
so come close and listen carefully.
You see, I'm a storyteller from days of old---
with lessons to reveal and stories to be told."

The Storyteller Collection

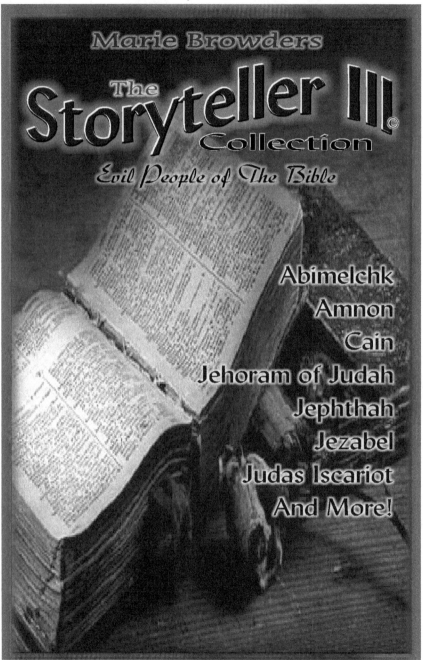

New Cover! New Theme!
Available 11/2018

The Storyteller Collection

Available Now!
Amazon.com
Barnes and Nobel

The Storyteller Collection

TALENTS
Marie Browders

Talent. It is any inherent ability or power that a person is endowed with naturally.

Talent implies an intrinsic ability for a specific pursuit or special ability bestowed upon a person. It is naturally acquired through no effort on anyone's part. It is inborn... innate. In other words, you are simply born with it.

Your talent is a special "gift" to you. A "present" from your "Benefactor", that is your "legacy", your "inheritance", and your "birthright".

Let me show you how to:
- Identify your talent.
- Use multiple talents together.
- Understand now and later talents.
- Turn your talents into financial solvency.

$14.95
ISBN 978-1-60702-415-6

pressions

9 781607 024156

Marie Browders'
"I Am!"
Series Book

We are now introducing all seven "I Am" books in one book! These character building books are designed to strengthen and direct children in a positive way. Each of these books come with a different message:

- What to do when challenged.
- How to make better decisions.
- How to deal with envy.
- What to do about lying.
- How to handle rivalry.
- How to stand up to prejudice.
- Recognizing what's safe and unsafe.

Barcode Area
We will add the barcode for you
Made with Cover Creator

Available Now!
Amazon.com

The Storyteller Collection

Marie Browders'

The Storyteller© Collection

Christmas Edition

A Beautiful Story
The Visitor
Letter from Satan
Death Row
Begin Again
Calvin
God's Wings
Million Dollar Bill
Blind
...and more!

Available
10/2018

CPSIA information can be obtained
at www.ICGtesting.com
Printed in the USA
LVHW081219271120
672805LV00035B/546